THE EMPEROR OF THE UNITED STATES OF AMERICA AND OTHER MAGNIFICENT BRITISH ECCENTRICS

'Until he ate a bluebottle, William Buckland had always maintained that the taste of mole was the most repulsive he knew.' So opens the portrait of William Buckland, the founder of geology and one of the most peculiar eccentrics featured in this remarkable and dazzlingly funny book. One hundred and four of the greatest British eccentrics are featured, and a greater galaxy of stars is difficult to imagine – Romeo Coates, the diamond-clad actor, who rewrote Shakespeare; John Christie, the founder of Glyndebourne, who for a time provided all female guests with knitting needles and wool; Simon Ellerton, who preferred walking with a large stone on his head; and, of course, the sublime poet, William McGonagall. Perhaps most astonishing is Joshua Norton, born in 1819, who reigned as Emperor of the United States of America for over twenty years. His Imperial Palace was only a small room in a seedy lodging house, but like all great eccentrics his ambitions were not constrained by the realities of everyday life.

THE EMPEROR OF THE UNITED STATES OF AMERICA AND OTHER MAGNIFICENT BRITISH ECCENTRICS

A CORGI BOOK 0 552 99007 8

Originally published in Great Britain
by Routledge & Kegan Paul Ltd.

PRINTING HISTORY

Routledge & Kegan Paul edition published 1981
Corgi edition published 1982

This book is set in 10/11 California

Corgi Books are published by
Transworld Publishers Ltd.,
Century House, 61–63 Uxbridge Road,
Ealing, London W5 5SA

Made and printed in Great Britain by
Guernsey Press Ltd, Guernsey,
Channel Islands.

The Emperor of The United States of America & other magnificent British eccentrics

Catherine Caufield

Drawings by Peter Till
Designed by Kate Hepburn

CORGI BOOKS
A DIVISION OF TRANSWORLD PUBLISHERS LTD

Contents

M

N

O

P

R

S

Acknowledgments

I owe thanks to a number of people whose advice and suggestions were invaluable to me in the writing of this book. First I must express my gratitude to the hundreds of biographers and diarists in whose works I discovered so many of the characters I have written about here.

Jay Bosworth, R D Boyle, Brent Elliot, Gillian Darley, Richard Ingrams, Michael Janson, Sir Osbert Lancaster, David Low, Anne Scott-James, Colin Ward and Julian Watson were all kind enough to bring to my attention eccentric characters of whom I should otherwise have remained sadly ignorant.

The innumerable County Librarians and Record Officers with whom I corresponded were unfailingly helpful, as were the local history societies, many of whose members went far beyond the call of duty in ploughing through old records to provide me with dates and anecdotes of local characters. In this connection I must mention with gratitude H A Beavin, Major J Coryton, and Audrey Strange.

Another marvellous source of information was the Church of England. I bombarded vicars all over the country with queries about their predecessors or past parishioners. The Reverend Mark Kennaway, Hugh Pickles, Kenneth Robinson, and John Preston were particularly helpful.

Among the many individuals who responded generously to my rather odd requests for information were Anne Crawshay, Magdalen Goffin, Susanna Graham-Jones,

Richard Hall, Marshall Kilduff, Leslie Marchand, Christopher Overton, David Pryce-Jones and Thomas Thorogood.

My thanks also to Gill Coleridge, David Godwin, Stratford Caldecott and Kate Hepburn for their advice and hard work in connection with the publication of this book.

Most of my research was done in the excellent London Library. Where else can one find a copy of the *Cork Historical and Archaeological Society Journal* for 1892 on the open shelves – and be allowed to take it home for a leisurely perusal? To Douglas Matthew, the Head Librarian, for his ability to unearth obscure references and his generosity in doing so, I am very much in debt.

Dr Peter McEwan and Professor Keith Thomas kindly discussed the theory and history of eccentric behaviour with me and their insights were most helpful as I groped for an understanding of the phenomenon.

I owe a special debt to my mother, also Catherine Caufield, also American, for passing on to me her delight in the English character.

Lastly, my thanks to Richard Boston for his kindness and good humour in reading the manuscript, his helpfulness in being ever on the *qui vive* for new eccentrics, and his patience in acting as a sounding-board throughout the writing of this book.

Introductions

The nucleus around which this book was formed was a short magazine article I wrote about Joshua Norton, the Englishman, who in 1859 proclaimed himself Emperor of the United States. The citizens of his adopted city, San Francisco, took Norton to their hearts, clothing him, accepting his homemade currency, and standing in tribute when he entered a restaurant or theatre.

The special appeal of Norton's story is in the warmth with which San Franciscans accepted his self-assigned role. The extent to which an individual or a society can tolerate or even encourage differentness is a significant measure of its strength, its confidence, its intelligence.

On ideological grounds alone, eccentricity has had a number of eloquent supporters. John Stuart Mill, in his essay, *On Liberty*, argued that, for as long as mankind is imperfect, different opinions and varieties of character should be given free scope as experiments in living. Diversity is a pre-condition of evolution, genetic or behavioural. Mill thought eccentricity desirable in an age of conformity, simply as an example of freedom. 'Eccentricity has always abounded when and where strength of character has abounded. . . . That so few now dare to be eccentric marks the chief danger of the time.'

Mill's conviction that eccentricity is an indication of strength of character was echoed by a *Times* leader in May 1966, on the occasion of the death of Colonel Wintle (see p. 214). 'Eccentricity may be impractical, uncomfortable, at times a nuisance. But it denotes character and individuality. It also pleases the escapist imp in all of us.'

The fact that eccentric behaviour is not always easy to live with, that it may be 'impractical, uncomfortable, at times a nuisance', may account for the widespread perception that true eccentricity is on the decline. A certain interval of time or distance may be necessary before we can recognise eccentricity as something other than inconvenient or offensive behaviour.

Having chosen my own eccentrics, so to speak, and known them for almost two years, I am extremely fond of most of them. Nevertheless, there are a number with whom I would not relish the prospect of living. George Mathew, who devoted himself to pleasing his friends, would surely have been a joy to know, but

11

the Earl of Bridgewater, serving formal dinners to his dogs and reading his will aloud to friends, must have been hard to bear. Had I lived in London in 1815 I would have been pleased to accept an invitation to one of William Kitchiner's Eta Beta Pi dinners, but having made my way through the filthy streets, I should probably have been turned away at the door for arriving one minute after the appointed hour.

Having constructed an elaborate system of social intercourse, we do not like to grant exemptions without some tangible benefit to ourselves. Geniuses and artists are often excused their irregularities (at least by the general public, as, once again, it is not so easy for those who have to live with them), in return for the fruits of their talents. Ordinary people are expected to abide by the rules. Most, indeed, are happy to do so. As Mill says of such people, again in *On Liberty*, 'I do not mean that they choose what is customary in preference to what suits their inclination. It does not occur to them to have any inclination, except what is customary.' The people in this book are not, for the most part geniuses. But they are strong individuals with inclinations of their own which they were not afraid to follow.

Not all unorthodox behaviour, of course, can be called eccentric. Categories such as eccentric, affected, fanatical, mad, and simply funny, blend imperceptibly into one another because, happily, human behaviour is not subject to precise delineations and measurements. *The Oxford English Dictionary's* definition of an eccentric as an irregular, odd or whimsical person is too vague to use as a yardstick. Many writers have included witches, freaks, criminals, madmen and rogues in their galleries of eccentric characters. I have chosen to write about what I call the pure eccentric, which might be defined as what is left over when the types mentioned above have been filtered out.

Eccentricity implies minor deviation. An object is eccentric when it is slightly off-course or off-centre. A violent rerouting of the path, a complete rejection of the old centre lifts the action out of eccentricity and into rebellion, criminality or madness.

Eccentrics, at least for my purposes, are also funny. They deviate from the norm in ways so odd and quirky that one wonders what made them think of it, not to mention what drove them to act out their ideas. One source of eccentric humour is the discrepancy between the strength of will needed to flout convention and the frivolous or inconsequential nature of the result. Like a blade of grass pushing through a concrete paving slab, the effect is incongruous and a little awe-inspiring. Thomas de Quincey, a great admirer of 'Walking Stewart' (see pp. 157–8), said of him that 'he was a man of genius, but not a man of talents; at least his genius was out of all proportion to his talents.'

Though eccentricity is an indication of character, the social prerequisite for eccentricity is a strong standardised code of conduct. In Britain, rules of behaviour that form the basis of our present code began to take shape in the fifteenth and sixteenth centuries. Deprived of real power by the development of a strong monarchy that took control of financial and military affairs into its own hands and of financial omnipotence by the growth of the merchant class, the aristocracy managed to retain its privileged position not by threat of force, but by developing distinctive patterns of behaviour that set it apart from the rest of the population.

Dress, language, humour and manners were some of the ways in which people made significant statements about themselves. Fashions in behaviour changed, of course – partly as a result of the upper class's struggle to maintain a distinct identity as aristocratic mores filtered through the rest of society. There was a tendency towards ever finer gradations of rank and increasingly restrictive behaviour. This codification provided a framework for maintaining social order (and social orders). It also gave an opportunity for an eccentric few, by following their own internal codes, to shock or amuse people and by their transgressions to define the limits of the public code. The word eccentric, according to *The Oxford English Dictionary*, was first used in a figurative sense, meaning odd or whimsical, in 1630.

The function of eccentricity as a rebellion against strict standards of social behaviour may also explain why there are relatively few records of female eccentricity. Because their role has been less public than men's, women have been less affected by public conventions. And, as irrational creatures, women have not been relied upon to uphold the logical, man-made social order. Small acts of female eccentricity are subsumed in the greater eccentricity of simply being female in a masculine world. It is not altogether astonishing that male writers have not paid close attention to nuances of behaviour of a group whose rules and actions they could not fully understand and which they thought unimportant.

To the extent to which eccentricity is an expression of individuality, it is a most unlikely attribute for a woman trained to submerge herself in the care of a husband and family. The same holds true for a labourer whose employment depends on his subservience and obedience to orders.

Eccentricity, however, is not merely a rich man's prerogative. It is the prerogative of those who can afford to step outside the system. Wealthy men are, of course, in a position to do this, but wealth alone is neither a sufficient nor a necessary condition for eccentric behaviour. There must be an internal impetus, an element of originality, of individuality, to distinguish eccentricity from a rich man's self-indulgence.

There are other types of people whose position in life make it easier, if they have the will, to ignore custom. Scholars, for example, and clergymen, though not necessarily wealthy, exist in institutions that both support and define them, giving them the freedom to behave in a contrary fashion. People with low expectations of society are also freer to act as they please. Tramps, recluses, Jacks of all trades, and, to a degree, literary men, who rely on their wits for a living, all fall into this category.

I have tried to explain why I selected these particular eccentrics, though readers will doubtless notice many omissions and quarrel with many inclusions. My defence must be that individual inclinations are so varied, so outlandish and so unpredictable that they defy all analysis. In the end, my choice is itself eccentric.

Alington
John

lington believed he had a responsibility to widen the horizons of the men who worked for him on Letchworth Estate. After their morning's work in the fields, he often brought a barrel of beer for them to drink as he read aloud from Shakespeare and the Bible. As part of this educational campaign, he decided to send his men up to London to see the Great Exhibition of 1851, but since none of them had ever been to the metropolis, Alington thought it best to rehearse them thoroughly beforehand. He had them lay out on the grounds of Letchworth a large-scale model of all the streets in London between Hyde Park and King's Cross, using logs felled from trees on the estate. For one week he drilled all his workers on the route from the railway station to the Exhibition and back again. Those pacing out the way to the Crystal Palace wore hay bands around their right legs, while those learning the return journey had bands around the left leg. This was meant to reduce confusion, but something seems to have gone wrong because, in the end, a disgusted Alington declared that they were all too thick to be trusted to find their way and the trip was cancelled.

During the Crimean War, Alington felt that his workers would benefit from having a clear idea of the fortifications at Sebastopol. Accordingly, the winter of 1855 was spent planning and constructing trenches, ramparts, and bastions on the estate in preparation for the re-enactment of the battle, with troops for both sides being drafted from the male population of Letchworth. Alington oversaw the work sitting on a platform in an old oak tree; once the battle began he used this position as a sniper's nest.

In an attempt to teach his men geography, Alington turned a small pond into a model of the world, constructing in it and along its edges, isthmuses, peninsulas, capes, islands, and continents. This they toured in rowing boats while Alington gave introductory lectures on the countries of the world, followed by discussions and quizzes.

There was plenty of time on the estate for diversions of this sort because under Alington's rule Letchworth, which he had inherited from his grandfather, was farmed for amusement, not profit. He kept no account books and the land produced only a fraction of its potential. Labourers were assigned odd jobs such as digging a series of holes one day and filling them up the next. Flint was laboriously picked out of the stony fields and piled into great columns which were dotted around the estate. This state of affairs pleased Alington because he had had a feud with Mr Knapp, the rector of Letchworth, and low productivity meant smaller tithes for his arch-enemy.

The quarrel came about when Mr Knapp objected to Alington's method of conducting services. Alington paid no attention to the correct order of prayer, substituting readings which – when they were not scandalous – were garbled. Finally, the bishop barred Alington from preaching at Letchworth.

Immediately Alington formed a breakaway congregation and began holding religious services at his house. These had Bacchanalian overtones, but sheer silliness also played a part. Prior to each service he rode up and down the aisles on his own contraption, a sort of four-wheeled bicycle, with a jar of snuff which he offered to members of the congregation at random.

The service proper began when Alington, wearing the leopard skin which served as his cassock, read the lesson – usually a short story and a love poem. Then came the sermon, passionate and unfathomable, which ended with Alington tearing off his wig in a frenzy, waving it about, and throwing it to the audience.

Six days a week – Saturday was his day of rest – Alington held open house. He was especially welcoming to tramps, gypsies and other outcasts. No one had to knock; those on horseback could ride up the steps and into the hall. Often visitors were treated to an impromptu performance by Alington at the piano in his leopard skin singing ribald songs.

Alington did have a number of quiet hobbies: he painted, sewed, and played hand bells. He also enjoyed being carried around his garden in an open coffin. An acquaintance who came upon him at one such moment heard Alington's voice issuing from the casket, 'You see,' he explained, 'I'm getting ready.'

Defiant to the end, Alington in his last illness refused to take the prescribed medicine until his gardener had tried it for three days. A second formula was offered, but Alington threw it to the ground. He called instead for a tumbler of brandy, drank it, and with a sigh fell back onto his pillow and died.

Badger
Harry

adger was a familiar figure in Cork during the early 1800s. Dressed in yellow buckskin trousers, a red coat of vaguely military cut, and a brass helmet bristling with iron spikes, he could generally be found lounging about near the old courthouse in South Main Street. His most celebrated characteristic was his placid indifference to what he ate or drank, and wagers were often laid on how far he could be persuaded to go. A mouse was once slipped into his pint of porter. Harry saw it, but raised no objection and calmly finished his drink. His last meal was a bowl of 'tripe' – actually strips of boiled leather in a milk and honey sauce. It took him two days to eat it. On the third day he died.

Bagenal
Beauchamp

Beauchamp Bagenal's behaviour on the Grand Tour astonished his contemporaries. According to Jonah Barrington he 'fought a prince, jilted a princess, intoxicated the Doge of Venice, carried off a Duchess from Madrid, scaled the walls of a convent in Lisbon, [and] concluded his exploits with a duel at Paris.' The jilted princess, Princess Charlotte of Mecklenburgh-Strelitz, consoled herself by marrying George III.

At home at Dunleckney, in County Carlow, 'King' Bagenal, as he was known, entertained a never-ending procession of guests and spongers on a grand scale. They repaid him by obedience to his whims, not always a simple task. Meals at Dunleckney were first and foremost drinking contests. At table, Bagenal kept a brace of pistols by his side. One was used to top the cask of claret that was consumed at each sitting, the other to ensure that no guest refused to drink his share.

The all-night revels that followed these dinners were compulsory. One guest, a clergyman, who realised that he could not keep up and hid in the grounds rather than be obliged to take part, described the scene the next morning when 'such of the company as were still able to walk' piled the bodies of their insensible companions onto a flatcar and delivered them to their respective homes.

In an age of obsessive duelling, Beauchamp Bagenal took second place to no man in his enthusiasm for a good fight. As Mr Neill O'Daunt put it, 'he had a tender affection for pistols. He was eager to pass his wisdom on to the younger generation, and derived great delight from encouraging the young men who frequented his house to hunt, drink, and solve points of honour at twelve paces.'

He even provoked his godson, Beauchamp Bagenal Harvey, to a duel. Harvey shot first and missed, whereupon Bagenal, immensely pleased, exclaimed, 'Damn you, you young rascal! Do you know that you had like to kill your godfather? Go back to Dunleckney, you dog, and have a good breakfast got ready for us. I only wanted to see if you were stout.'

Bagenal was lame and preferred to lean against a tombstone when fighting a duel. His last duel, however, was fought from an entirely new position. In order to provoke a quarrel, he sent an insulting note to a neighbour whose pigs had strayed onto his land. In due course he received a challenge to which he attached one condition before accepting. Because he was sixty he claimed the right to face his opponent from an armchair. The outcome was that his neighbour was seriously wounded, the arm of the chair was shattered, and Bagenal was unhurt.

Baring
Maurice

For a man whose profession was literature, Maurice Baring showed little respect for the printed page. Whenever a passage in a book struck him, Baring simply cut it out and pasted it in one of his notebooks. Baring accumulated a good many books in his seventy years of life, but each time he moved house – a not infrequent occurrence with him – he gave his entire library away and started collecting from scratch in his new residence. So much simpler, he explained, than moving all those books.

He was never without books, however, and had enough to

spare for friends in need. When Sir Ronald Stows lost all his books in a fire in Cyprus, he received a telegram: 'Sending library. Maurice.' Soon after there arrived 'a small but heavy chest', Baring's travelling library stocked with miniature editions of the classics in seven languages.

Baring was quite unconcerned with material possessions. A friend, accompanying him on a train journey through Germany was astonished to see Baring, having failed to fit a new overcoat into his holdall, throw it out the window without pausing in his conversation.

Baring was a man of wide interests. He embarked on a diplomatic career in 1899, but abandoned it in favour of being a war correspondent. In 1912 *The Times* sent him to cover the fighting in the Balkans. Action was sporadic and Baring disliked idleness so, to the surprise of his editor, he alternated his war despatches with drama reviews and commentaries on Eastern literature.

He developed a language of his own, which he used as if other people shared it with him. A notice appeared one morning in the personal columns of *The Times*: 'Wumble, humble sumble 1851'. Luckily, a member of the vast Baring clan decoded it and sent Maurice an 1851 half-sovereign.

Always fond of children, Baring had a childish streak himself. On his birthday he usually jumped fully clothed into the nearest large body of water. This ritual was performed at Windsor, Brighton, Killarney, Seville, and Copenhagen, among other places. Baring also enjoyed giving children's parties and entertaining his friends' children – not always as the parents might have wished. One quiet and obedient little girl turned into a monster after an outing with Baring, so much so that her parents, unable to explain her behaviour in any other way, feared she was ill. Finally it came out that Baring had bribed her with five shillings to be 'as naughty as possible'.

Barrett
John

Barrett was a vice-provost and professor of oriental languages at Trinity College, Dublin. He spoke and wrote Latin and Greek fluently, but his English was appalling. In the words of a contemporary, Barrett was 'so ignorant of his own [language] that his conversation was a tissue of blunders and grammatical absurdities.' He once translated *Gallia est omnis divisa in partes tres* as 'all Gaul is quartered into three halves.' None the less, Barrett's classical and philological learning was profound and he was a devoted scholar. One of his great achievements was the discovery, hidden in a later manuscript, of an ancient Greek text of the Gospel of St Matthew when he noticed, as he put it, 'a dear little iota in the corner'.

Barrett invariably lectured to a capacity crowd, but this may be partly attributable to his reputation for cursing and swearing. He was a pious man and serious about his religion, but practically every sentence he uttered was studded by colourful expletives not at the time common in academic circles.

Learned as he was in matters academic, Barrett was almost unbelievably ignorant when it came to everyday life. He had entered Trinity in 1767 as a student at the age of fourteen and spent the rest of his life behind its walls, normally leaving campus only three times a year – once to Dunsink, a Dublin suburb, for the Fellows' annual outing and twice across the road to collect his dividends from the Bank of Ireland.

On one occasion, when he did venture to dine outside College, he and his companions passed a flock of grazing sheep. Barrett, mystified, asked what they were and was delighted to discover that he was looking at 'live mutton'. He was scarcely less ignorant about women. After dinner on the same occasion, when the guests were drinking the health of their ladies, the host asked Barrett to propose his 'belle'. He replied with innocent gallantry, 'I'll give you the College bell; for I'm told she's finer than Big Tom of Lincoln.'

Barrett, who owned two cats and was noted for his inability to apply logic to commonplace problems, is the original of the following story which has been attributed to various people. A visiting friend noticed two holes at the bottom of Barrett's door and asked what they were for. To let the cats in and out, explained his host.

'Why', said the visitor, 'would not one do for both?'

'You silly man, how could the big cat get into the little hole?', replied Barrett.

'But could not the little one go through the big hole?'

'Egad,' said the doctor, 'and so she could, but I never thought of that.'

Hearing that the College was going to pay to have some rubble carted away, Barrett proposed a money-saving scheme. Why not just dig a hole and bury the rubble? When asked what would be done with the earth from the hole, Barrett answered, 'D'ye see me now, can't you dig another hole and bury that?'

As a well-known Trinity character, 'Jacky' Barrett was regarded with a mixture of affection and pride by the rest of his college but this did not rule out a certain urge to tease him. His dirty clothes, filthy hands and face earned him the nickname 'Sweep'.

Barrett was a good-natured and generous man, but close when it came to money matters. He lived frugally, augmenting his salary by collecting and selling old candle ends, thus amassing a considerable fortune. However, rather than go to the expense of a fire in his room, Barrett would sneak down and sit before the kitchen fire – a habit which was halted when the servants raised objections to his ragged appearance.

Another of Barrett's little economies was to powder his own hair on special occasions to save the expense of a wig. Before bed, he would carefully comb the powder out onto a sheet of paper and save it for the next ceremony. He dined in Hall because it was free and during the day limited himself to a half-penny's worth each of bread and milk. These were fetched for him by his servant of many years, Catty. One day she slipped, injuring herself seriously, and was taken to hospital. Barrett was grieved at the plight of his old friend and hurried to see her. After inquiring how she felt and expressing his sympathy, he recollected himself and asked 'D'ye hear, Catty, where's the jug?' 'Oh, doctor, dear, sure the jug was broke and I couldn't help it.' 'Very good, Catty, that's true, it couldn't be helped; but, d'ye see me now, where's my halfpenny change?'

Barrett-Lennard
Sir Thomas

It is not uncommon for a country squire of ancient lineage to have his own family cemetery, but in Sir Thomas Barrett-Lennard's neatly laid out burial grounds at Belhus in Essex, the plots were reserved exclusively for animals. Funeral services for the dogs, cats, and horses who made up a major part of Sir Thomas's entourage were conducted by the vicar of nearby Aveley. A footman bearing aloft a miniature coffin, led Sir Thomas in a long white gown, and the vicar to the graveside for the solemn rites.

Sir Thomas's love of animals was not restricted to pets. Workers on the estate were under order to keep a fresh bowl of water in the corn rick for the rats, and it was strictly forbidden to harm any members of Belhus's thriving rodent population. If a rat had to be disturbed at all, it was put in a sack, taken to the edge of the woods and released.

Unlike many an animal lover, Sir Thomas was kind to humans as well. Rather than disturb his butler, he often answered the door himself, with the result that many visitors to Belhus were initially shocked to find themselves admitted to so fine a house by so shabby an attendant. As the years passed Sir Thomas's interest in his appearance declined, and on several occasions he received tips from strangers on the estate who mistook him for a gatekeeper. There were, however, more awkward moments. In 1900 Sir Thomas was the chairman of the Essex Asylum Committee and while returning from a meeting at a local institution one evening, he decided to take a short cut through some woods and fields. He was stopped by a policeman who found his appearance and presence in the area suspicious.

'Where are you going?' the officer demanded.

'To Belhus.'

'And where have you come from?'

'Brentwood Lunatic Asylum.'

'Knew it!' cried the officer and the 'escaped patient' was handcuffed and transported back to the Asylum. Finally, after much discussion, the policeman was persuaded of his error and Sir Thomas was allowed to return to his study where he could once again indulge in his hobbies of constructing riddles in Latin and translating nonsense poems into Greek.

Beauclerk
Osborne de Vere

'Obby', as his friends called him, took little part in public life; in fact, his forays into that arena seem mostly to have been motivated by a gleeful desire to cause havoc. He held the hereditary post of Grand Falconer and proposed attending the 1953 Coronation with a live falcon on his wrist. When the organisers suggested a stuffed bird instead, he boycotted the ceremony. Parishioners at the church near his home in Ireland remember him snoozing through sermons with a handkerchief over his face, rousing himself occasionally to shout out, 'Rubbish!'

He married late in life and never had any legitimate children, partly for fear of passing on a streak of madness that ran in his branch of the family. About illegitimate children, however, he had no such inhibitions, and boasted of having large numbers of them, although, unlike the 9th Earl of Orford who kept track of his by insisting that they all be named Horatio Walpole, Obby professed to be unsure of exactly how many he had. On one occasion a certain baronet and his wife who were lunching with the Duke were mystified to hear him repeatedly muttering to a friend in very audible asides, 'What do you think? Is he one of mine?'

His sense of decorum was strict, if unpredictable. Once, when his wife was late coming down to a lunch, Obby gave her seat to a man who had come to check the fire extinguishers and when she did appear he refused to allow her to join the table. He expected the hall porter at his club, Brooks's, to wind his watch for him, holding out his arm and saying, 'There's a good fellow'. Once, while he was eating in a hotel restaurant, a fire broke out. The Duke remained at his table and when urged by the waiters to escape, he replied, 'Nonsense! Bring me some more toast.' On the other hand the ducal dignity was allowed to slip rather badly when on a visit to Lord Dunraven he arrived carrying only a toothbrush and a pair of pyjamas in a brown paper bag.

Obby lived to the age of eighty-nine, with little thought of growing old gracefully. At eighty-three he took a freighter to the US, crossed the country by Greyhound bus, and toured Latin America, travelling second class all the way. A newspaper interview two years previously in which he expressed a desire for a young wife brought him sixty-eight offers of marriage, including a number of titled and highly eligible ladies. He opted for continued singleness, the state in which eccentricity and crotchetiness best thrive.

Beckford
William

From the age of ten when his father died, leaving him an estate worth £1,000,000 and an annual income of over £100,000, William Beckford was one of the wealthiest people in Britain. He was also an only child, educated at home, with only his tutors and nurses for company. Beckford found release from this lonely existence in an obsessive fascination with the East.

By his twenty-first year Beckford had written his masterpiece, *Vathek*, an oriental romance, as well as several lesser works. But his romantic posturing and artistic pretensions made him an object of suspicion among his social peers. In 1783 his family, alarmed by rumours of an improper relationship between him and William Courtenay, a young family friend, pressured Beckford into marrying Lady Margaret Gordon. Two years later they left England for Geneva, but the scandalous stories followed him and even in exile Beckford was ostracised. His wife, with whom he had in fact been very happy, died the following year and Beckford was left quite alone.

He spent the next fifteen years travelling, a conspicuous figure, accompanied as he was by his doctor, his *maître d'hôtel*, baker, cook, valet, three footmen and twenty-four musicians, not to mention his bed, cutlery, plate, books and prints. He required any inn at which he stopped to have his rooms repapered for him, and on one occasion, while in Portugal, imported a flock of sheep from England to improve the view from his window.

From time to time Beckford returned to England to oversee improvements at Fonthill, the family home in Wiltshire. In 1799 he retired permanently to Fonthill in order to indulge a newly discovered passion for building.

To keep out prying eyes Beckford first surrounded his estate with a 7-mile long, 12-foot high wall topped with iron spikes. He then settled down to some serious building, beginning with an elaborate folly, 'a convent, partly in ruins and partly perfect', next to the existing house at Fonthill. Later Beckford's fevered imagination suggested a much more grandiose scheme: he instructed his architect, James Wyatt, to build a complete abbey, with a 300-foot high octagonal tower, in which he could live.

So that its effect could be properly studied, the tower was first constructed out of wood. This was toppled and a permanent one built in its place. Not very permanent, however, because Wyatt had been under such pressure from the impatient Beckford that it was erected too hastily, using shoddy materials and the inadequate foundations of an old summer house. Within a few months, it collapsed. A third tower, this time of brick and stone, but still on a weak foundation, was built. Beckford was so eager to see the edifice completed that he bribed his workmen to work in relays through the night, seven days a week by supplying them with ample quantities of food and ale. The result of this was that most of Fonthill Abbey was built by men who were in an advanced state of intoxication.

Beckford's impatience was legendary. Once he conceived an idea he could not bear any delay in realising it. If he expressed a wish to ride along a certain path in his woods, he expected to find the trail cleared the following morning, even if the whole village had to be mobilised to work all night. At one point the distracted Wyatt had to divert 500 men from working on a job for George III at Windsor to Fonthill. When he was an old man Beckford commented, 'I like to be among workmen. I never kept less than 100 at one time when at Fonthill.'

In 1800 Beckford determined to have Christmas dinner in the Abbey and in spite of the fact that the mortar in the kitchen was still wet and the beams not securely in place, he did so. As the last of the servants carried the last of the food to the dining-room, the kitchen collapsed behind him. Luckily no one was injured. Rebuilding began immediately.

Beckford had very little company at Fonthill. Apart from his Spanish dwarf, his doctor, and his heraldic advisor, his closest companions were his dogs: Viscount Fartleberry, Mrs Fry, Nephew and Tring. On occasion he would order a magnificent dinner for twelve and, with twelve servants attending, sit down alone, eat one dish, and then rise from the table. Generally, though, he lived quite simply, spending money not on clothes or parties, but on Fonthill itself.

In 1807 Beckford sold the old house and moved lock, stock and barrel into the Abbey. In spite of all the expense in building it (estimates of its cost vary from *The Times*'s £1,000,000 to Beckford's own £273,000) Fonthill Abbey was not a very comfortable place to live. Most of its rooms were higher than wide, ill-lit, and ill-ventilated. Still, there were plenty of people who wanted to see it.

One man, a cousin of the painter, W P Frith, scaled the outer wall on a wager. He was shown around the gardens and the house by someone he took to be the gardener. His guide, however, proved to be Beckford himself who, far from behaving like the ogre he had been painted, invited the intruder to dinner and was a charming host. After a sumptuous meal, Beckford excused himself and was gone for some time. Finally a servant came in, escorted the man to the door, and said, 'Mr Beckford ordered me to present his compliments to you, sir, and I am to say that as you found your way into Fonthill Abbey without assistance, you may find your way out as best you can; and he hopes you will take care to avoid the bloodhounds that are let loose in the garden every night.' Beckford's 'guest' spent a sleepless night sitting in the branches of a tree. The next morning he scaled the wall to safety and never set foot inside Fonthill again.

In 1822 financial reverses forced Beckford to sell the Abbey, still uncompleted. He parted quite calmly with what had been his major interest in life for over twenty-two years, saying that it had only been a plaything. John Farquhar, a businessman, paid £300,000 for the estate. Three years later the Great Tower collapsed. Although there were people inside the Abbey at the time, no one noticed it crumbling until the dust began pouring in through the windows. The building materials were so flimsy that the fall had been almost silent. Farquhar took the disaster in his stride, commenting that it made Fonthill a more manageable size.

Beckford removed to Bath and began work on another tower on Lansdown Crescent. Rumours about him abounded. It was said that he hated women and had niches built into the walls so that maids could hide as he went past. When he went out for an excursion he was accompanied by a steward, four grooms and six or more yapping dogs.

His new tower, 130 feet high, crowned with a cast-iron model of the temple of Lysicrates, and incorporating a chapel and library, was set in a garden-cum-graveyard. His dog, Tiny, was buried there in a marble tomb and in 1844 William Beckford, too, was laid to rest there in a pink granite sarcophagus.

5th Duke of Portland
Bentinck-Scott
William John Cavendish

The 5th duke of Portland was a gentle recluse with a mania for building. In his younger days as MP for King's Lynn from 1824–6 he had known something of public life, but he withdrew more and more from society until at the end of his life he went out only at night, his way lit by a lamp carried by an old woman who kept forty yards in front of him.

The Duke's chief interest was the improvement of Welbeck Abbey, his estate in Nottinghamshire. After his accession to the dukedom in 1854 he was absorbed with planning and supervising his building schemes, most of which were carried out underground. At his death there were 15,000 men employed on 36 different projects at Welbeck. In addition to good wages, each employee was given a donkey and an umbrella, but there was one important condition of employment: the workers were not to speak to or acknowledge the Duke. In the words of one local contemporary, 'the man who touched his hat was discharged.' This injunction applied also to his tenants, his doctor and the local parson.

One of his additions to Welbeck was the largest private apartment in England, an underground ballroom 174 feet long, large enough for 2000 people. It was served by a huge lift that could carry twenty people at a time. Thousands of gas jets supplemented the natural illumination offered by rows of mushroom-shaped skylights. Like the rest of the subterranean apartments, the ballroom was centrally heated. Other underground chambers included a series of libraries, one of which had space for twelve full-sized billiard tables; and the Rose Corridor, a long glass-roofed conservatory onto which all the rooms opened. The Duke had these and all the apartments at Welbeck painted pink.

There was also an underground railway to carry the Duke's

food the 150 yards from the kitchen to his diningroom; a tunnel wide enough to allow two carriages to travel abreast for the 1¼-mile journey to the nearest village, Worksop; and miles of ancillary underground passages linking various buildings on the estate. Above ground stood the largest riding-school in Europe – its walls covered in mirrors, its ceilings hung with crystal chandeliers. The Duke also built more than forty neo-Tudor lodges on the estate.

But no balls were ever given in the ballroom, nor billiards played in the library, and the ninety-four horses kept in the stables grew fat from lack of exercise because the Duke invited no one to visit him at Welbeck.

However, one of his improvements, the skating-rink, did get a good deal of use. In the words of Ottoline Morrell, half-sister to the 6th Duke, 'the Duke wished his house-maids to skate, and if he found one of them sweeping the corridor or stairs, the frightened girl was sent out to skate whether she wanted to or not.'

The Duke used only four or five of the many rooms at Welbeck. The rest were completely devoid of furniture or decoration, apart from the inevitable coat of pink paint. One of his rooms was lined from floor to ceiling with cupboards filled with green bandboxes, each of which contained one brown wig. Moreover, it was said that the Duke was not a stranger to false moustaches, beards, whiskers, and eyebrows.

His dress was likewise dictated by a desire for privacy. He wore three frock coats, made to fit one over the other, with colour-coded button tabs. His trousers were always tied at the bottom with a piece of string and his hat was almost two feet high. He was never without a large umbrella and a bulky overcoat, the better to hide himself from strangers.

The Duke travelled in a specially designed carriage with sunken seats and curtains at all the windows. He even managed to make the trip to London by train without being seen. With curtains drawn, the carriage was loaded onto a special railway car at Worksop and driven off when the train reached London.

Portland carried his self-imposed isolation so far that he twice refused an offer of the Garter because acceptance would have required him to appear at Court. On those occasions when medical attention was necessary, the doctor had to stand outside the sickroom questioning, diagnosing and even taking the patient's temperature through the medium of his valet. Those few who did have contact with the Duke spoke of him as a kind and intelligent man. A generous subscriber to charities, large and small, he sent a shipload of food and drink to British troops during the Crimean War and when Turkey was at war with Russia he donated £4,000 to hospitals there. Local children remembered him tossing coins to them as his carriage passed by, though they never saw his face. Some people believed that his passion for building stemmed from his desire to give employment to workers during hard times and that he built underground so as not to appear ostentatious. Whatever his original inspiration, the Duke's construction projects were almost his sole occupation. Collecting art was a minor passion with him, but in this too he was unconventional. He acquired many fine paintings for Welbeck, but one day made a bonfire out of several hundred that he deemed unfit for his collection. When the 6th Duke came to Welbeck after inheriting the title from his uncle, he found unframed paintings stacked two and three deep all around the huge riding school and a rare Gobelins tapestry rolled up and packed with peppercorns in an old tin box.

The strangest episode concerning the 5th Duke began seventeen years after his death. In 1896, a Mrs Annie Marie Druce claimed that her father-in-law, T C Druce, owner of a dry-goods store in Baker Street, had staged a mock funeral in 1864 and slipped back into his true identity as William John Cavendish Bentinck-Scott, 5th Duke of Portland. If the Duke had, as she claimed, been masquerading as a shopkeeper then Druce's son, her late husband, would have been the rightful 6th Duke and she herself the Dowager Duchess. For eleven years she and other members of the Druce family pursued this claim through the courts (complicated by the sudden appearance from Australia of someone claiming to be the long-lost eldest son of T C Druce).

The various claimants to the title financed their cases by selling shares in the Druce-Portland Company, investors in which were to be repaid out of the vast Portland wealth if and when the Druces succeeded to the Dukedom. Finally, T C Druce's coffin was opened and his body found inside, which, since the Duke's body was also found inside *his* coffin, proved they were two different people. The Druce claim was denied and most of the witnesses who supported it were convicted of perjury.

Beswick
Hannah

Miss Beswick of Cheetwood Hall, Manchester, suffered from a
morbid obsession much in vogue in the eighteenth century – the
fear of being buried alive. To prevent this, she left her doctor,
Charles White, £25,000 on condition that he visit her regularly
after her death.

Accordingly, when in 1758 she died, Dr White had Miss
Beswick embalmed, and placed her at the top of his house in a
grandfather-clock case, the glass front of which was draped
with a velvet curtain. Each year, on the anniversary of her
death, he paid her a morning visit accompanied by a witness.

When Dr White himself died in 1813, Miss Beswick was
moved to the Lying-In Hospital (now St Mary's) and thence to
the Manchester Museum of Natural History. When the museum
transferred to new premises in the mid-nineteenth century, Miss
Beswick was examined and the trustees came to the unanimous
decision that she was unmistakably dead. On 22 July 1868, she
was buried in the Manchester General Cemetery. No stone
marked her grave and the location is now lost to us.

'The Dinton Hermit'
Bigg
John

Known as the Dinton Hermit, John Bigg spent the last thirty-
odd years of his life in a cave at Dinton, Buckinghamshire. He
never begged, but lived on the free charity of local people, who
brought him food and drink without being asked.

There was only one thing John Bigg ever asked for – leather
scraps. These he immediately nailed onto his clothes, the
original fabric of which had long since disintegrated. One of
Bigg's shoes, made up of over 1000 pieces of leather is in the
Ashmolean Museum, Oxford.

John Bigg had at one time been a man of some standing – clerk
to Simon Mayne (one of the judges who passed sentence on

Charles I), tolerably wealthy, and something of a scholar. It was Charles II's restoration to the throne in 1660 that caused Bigg to fall into the deep melancholy from which he never recovered and which drove him to become a recluse. His case is the perfect counterpart to that of Sir Thomas Urquhart (*q.v.*) in whom the Restoration gave rise to an uncontrollable and ultimately fatal fit of laughter.

Birch
Thomas

Thomas Birch, a keeper of books at the British Museum in the mid-eighteenth century, was a keen fisherman with a novel method of attracting fish to his line. Disguising himself as a tree, he would take root by the side of a stream in a costume carefully designed to transform his arms into branches and the fishing line into a spray of blossom. Any movement would, he argued, be taken by the fish to be the natural effects of a mild breeze.

Although Birch was eventually discouraged from this approach by the ridicule of his friends, Sir Humphrey Davy (1778–1829) hit on a similar idea over half a century later. His fishing outfit consisted of a green coat, green breeches and an old green hat. 'In this attire,' wrote Cordy Jeafferson, 'Davy flattered himself he resembled vegetable life as closely as it was possible for mortal to do.'

On shooting expeditions, Davy adopted the opposite approach to dress. He tried to be as conspicuous as possible so as not to be shot by mistake. Usually he wore a large, broad-brimmed scarlet hat, though as one wag pointed out, this headgear put him in danger of being deliberately shot by an anti-cleric who mistook him for a cardinal. Davy always claimed he had no time for washing or changing his clothes. Instead he simply wore clean clothes over his dirty ones, sometimes wearing five shirts and five pairs of stockings.

Blackhurst
Ivy Mabel

Ivy Mabel Blackhurst, of Beauchief, Sheffield, left £20,000 to her cat, Blackie. For three years, until her death in 1978 at the age of eighteen, Blackie lived on in Mrs Blackhurst's detached house, waited on by a full-time housekeeper.

Bowles
Thomas Gibson

When in 1887 Thomas Gibson Bowles, the founder and publisher of the *Lady* and *Vanity Fair*, was left a widower with four children under the age of ten, he decided on a severely practical approach to the new task of childrearing. Health, he decided, was the most important thing. Bowles had studied some statistics that suggested that Jewish children were less susceptible to epidemic diseases than others. From then on his children were fed according to strict Mosaic law.

The dressing of girl children seemed to him an unnecessarily complicated matter, so he decided to have his daughters outfitted by the naval tailor who made his sons' clothes. As a result Sydney and Dorothy Bowles wore thick blue serge naval uniforms and sailor's caps until the age of seventeen.

In her teens, Sydney, later Lady Redesdale, the mother of the remarkable Mitford girls, had to endure a great deal of teasing from small boys who made fun of her odd clothes. At last her father was persuaded to allow her to dress in a manner more becoming a young woman. He consulted a friend, an actress who affected very dramatic costumes. With her help, a long, low-necked black velvet gown with a red sash and a large befeathered Duchess of Devonshire hat was selected as the seventeen-year-old Sydney's morning walking costume.

Cap'en Tommy, as the cartoonists called him, had strict views on the correct way to take a bath. He dismissed the conventional method as merely 'sitting in dirty water'. Instead, he took steam baths at his London club. When the family went to Scotland on holiday, however, he had to improvise, using some dog kennels in front of the house as a temporary Turkish bath. Bowles would sit steaming inside the first kennel, which had been lined with hot bricks, before emerging into the run where the butler was waiting on the roof of the next kennel to shower him with bucketfuls of cold water. From his position on the roof the butler could also announce the approach of any strangers whose sensibility might not be equal to the spectacle.

Bowles was MP for King's Lynn from 1892 to 1906. In 1899 he announced to his daughter, Dorothy, who was by now keeping house for him at their home in Lowndes Square, that he was fed up with politics and intended to move to China. Asked when he was thinking of taking this dramatic step, he replied, 'On Thursday. You'd better close up the house and pack.' Dorothy did as she was told; she said goodbye to her houseguests, had the furniture covered in dust sheets, arranged for a caretaker to look after the house, and at eleven o'clock on Thursday morning was sitting in Lowndes Square in a four-wheeled carriage, with all her luggage, waiting for her father to join her on the first leg of their journey. As Bowles came down the front steps a few raindrops fell; he lent in at the window of the cab and said, 'My dear child, it's raining. We won't go.'

'The Musical Small-coal Man'
Britton
Thomas

Thomas Britton was born in Northamptonshire, but came to London at an early age, and by 1677 he had established himself near Clerkenwell Green as a small-coal (charcoal) dealer, living with his wife above the old stable from which he conducted his business.

To this miserable dwelling, accessible only by an outside ladder, came well-known musicians and members of fashionable society, all eager to attend or perform at one of Britton's musical evenings. These began in 1678 when he founded a musical club with a number of friends and they continued every Thursday evening until his death nearly forty years later.

The quality of the concerts was such that they quickly acquired a reputation outside Britton's club and began to attract the best amateur and professional musicians of the day, including Handel. Doubtless, Britton's collections of ancient and modern music and of musical instruments were extra inducements. His harpsicord was said to be the best in Europe. On the other hand, Handel was content to play a 5-stop organ at one of Britton's evenings. Britton himself, while perhaps not up to the standards of some of his guests, frequently performed on the viola da gamba.

Not only musicians but leaders of society, including the Duchess of Queensbury, were happy to manoeuvre the rickety steps that led to the less-than-elegant 'concert room'. At first these evenings were free, but later there was a subscription of 10s a year with coffee served at 1d a dish.

Encouraged by his neighbour, Dr Garencieres, who was physician to the French Embassy, Britton became interested in chemistry. He built an ingenious movable laboratory which was much admired.

He achieved greater recognition, however, as a bibliophile, acting as agent and advisor to many wealthy collectors. Every Saturday in winter a group of enthusiasts, including the Duke of Devonshire and the Earls of Oxford, Pembroke and Winchelsea, wandered through London in search of books and met afterwards at the bookshop of Christopher Bateman in Paternoster Row. Often Britton joined them there, still wearing his blue coal-smock after a morning of selling coal in the streets, to discuss rare and valuable books. Britton formed and sold to Lord Somers the collection of pamphlets now known as the Somers' Tracts and he was involved in the formation of the Harleian Library which is now part of the British Library.

Britton's own collection of books was weighted towards the occult sciences and he was particularly interested in Rosicrucian philosophy, with which some of his chemical experiments may have been connected. He was also a very superstitious man, a characteristic that led to his death.

A Mr Robe, who often attended the Thursday-evening concerts, brought with him one night a ventriloquist, with the aim of fooling the superstitious Britton. The ventriloquist, a blacksmith named Honeyman, had some fame as 'the talking smith', but was unknown to his host. Throwing his voice, he announced in solemn tones that Britton would die at once unless he fell on his knees and recited the Lord's Prayer. Terrified, Britton obeyed instantly, but the shock so unnerved him that he soon took to his bed and died within a few days. He left little money, but his fine collections of music, instruments and books fetched high prices when they were sold at auction. His funeral on 1 October 1714 was attended by a large crowd and he was buried in a vault in St James, Clerkenwell, but no monument has ever marked the spot.

Because of his interests and acquaintances above his station, Britton was often the object of rumours to the effect that he was a Jesuit, a Presbyterian, an atheist or worse and that his concerts were less than innocent gatherings. The truth is that he was a plain, cheerful, honest man, much liked and admired by those who knew him. The painting of Thomas Britton by Woolaston now in the National Portrait Gallery shows a man with an open countenance, dressed in the clothes of the trade he pursued all his life and which, with all his accomplishments, he never thought beneath him.

Countess of Cardigan
Brudenell
Adeline

By living openly with Lord Cardigan for a year before they were married, Adeline Brudenell outraged Victorian society. As Lady Cardigan she became a leader of the 'fast' set, but the Queen never forgave her her youthful indiscretion. In 1873 Adeline's second marriage to a Portuguese nobleman, the Comte de Lancastre, gave her an opportunity for revenge. She continued to smoke in public, and to go cycling in tight red military trousers and leopard-skin cape, but she now had the added satisfaction of knowing that the gossips had anglicised her name to the 'Countess of Lancaster', Queen Victoria's own travelling pseudonym.

Lady Cardigan cut a no less distinctive figure in old age. An excellent rider in her day, she continued to attend all important meets in full hunting-dress. She had no intention, however, of actually joining in: her invariable custom was to step out of her carriage, look round anxiously, and with a sigh of exasperation declare that her incompetent groom must have taken her horse to the wrong meet. She was then free to enjoy the hunt as an onlooker.

In her last years Lady Cardigan was a memorable sight as she promenaded in Hyde Park, wearing a curly blonde wig, a three-cornered hat, a Louis XVI coat, and trailing her leopard skin behind. She was generally arm-in-arm with an elderly swain and followed at a respectful distance by a tall footman supporting her pet dog on a silk cushion.

She always loved entertaining, but developed some individual notions as to what it involved. It was one thing to dress up in mantilla and layered skirts and to dance and play the castanets, even if few other seventy-year-old ladies went in for

such activities. But her guests had also to humour her whim that Deene, the Cardigan home in Northamptonshire, was haunted by the ghost of a nun, and were expected to oblige by screaming and fainting when Lady Cardigan herself donned a nun's habit and drifted through the dimly lit reception rooms. One especially charming woman endeared herself to her hostess by fainting in earnest.

For several years before her death, Lady Cardigan kept a coffin in the ballroom at Deene. Assisted by the butler, she would from time to time climb in to make sure it was comfortable. The servants were summoned to these rehearsals of her lying-in-state and afterwards required to give their impressions of the overall effect.

Buckland
Francis Trevelyan

On July 12 1862, the Society for the Acclimatisation of Animals in the United Kingdom (the aim of which was to introduce new animals to Britain to ease food shortages) held a formal dinner in Willis's Rooms, London. The bill of fare included bird's nest soup, Japanese sea-slug, kangaroo (steamed and boiled), wild boar, curassow, and leporine. To one member, at least, this menu would not have seemed out of the ordinary. Frank Buckland, one of the founders of the Society, had a habit of eating strange foods. Boiled and fried slices of porpoise head, rhinoceros pie, panther chops, garden snails, slug soup, earwigs, and mice on toast were among his culinary experiences. He came by his curiosity (and his apparently cast-iron stomach) honestly. His father, William Buckland (*q.v.*) had often presided over a meal of crocodile steak, roast joint of bear, hedgehog and (in the interests of scientific experimentation) puppy.

Some of Frank Buckland's harshest comments were reserved for horsemeat. After a Horseflesh Dinner at the Langham Hotel, featuring horse tongue, soup, and sausage, as well as joints, boiled withers, and roast baron of horse, Buckland, who tasted everything, pronounced, 'in my humble opinion, hippophagy had not the slightest chance of success in this country.'

41

Buckland was a leading light of the Piscatorial Society, became Inspector of Salmon Fisheries, and created the Buckland Museum of Economic Fish Culture. More endearingly, perhaps, he was the author of *Curiosities of Natural History*, whose four volumes contain such helpful hints as the following: 'People who wish to have relics kept of favourite horses should have their ears preserved. They make nice holders for spills; the hoofs also make good inkstands; and the tails mounted on a stick are an excellent thing to kill flies.'

Frank's interest in natural curiosity extended to human beings. He befriended, and took an uncondescending interest in, giants, dwarfs, side-show freaks, and circus people, including Zazel, famous in her time as 'the beautiful lady shot from a monstrous cannon'. His friends also included rat-catcher, taxidermists, pet-shop owners, and collectors. Buckland acquired a great deal of practical knowledge from these men, accompanying them on excursions in and around London. How many other men of science could or would acknowledge the assistance in preparing a paper of 'Mr Shaw of ratcatching notoriety'?

With naturalists and circus performers constantly coming and going, Buckland's house was never dull. A relative of Mrs Buckland, who as a small child often visited the Buckland home, told her grandson, the zoologist John Napier, the following story: Descending a dark staircase, she tripped over a soft object and slid to the bottom. The object turned out to be a dead infant hippopotamus which had been placed there through lack of space elsewhere. Frank Buckland picked her up, dusted her down and admonished her with the words: 'You should be more careful. You might have damaged it. Hippopotamuses don't grow on trees, you know.'

Buckland maintained a sizeable and unusual menagerie. Apart from the conventional household pets, he also gave a home to a succession of African mongooses, all named Jemmy; a South African Red River Hog called Dick; a jackal; a racoon; an eagle; a buzzard; and a bear.

The bear, named Tiglath-Pileser, lived at Oxford while Frank was a student at Christ Church there. He acquired his name (an Assyrian king mentioned in the Bible) when he ambled into chapel and so startled the student who was reading the lesson that the last spoken words, Tiglath-Pileser, froze on the student's lips. On another occasion, Tig, dressed as usual in a cap and gown, was taken to a garden party, introduced to various celebrities, including Napoleon's nephew, and at

Florence Nightingale's instigation, was hypnotised and fell into a deep sleep within minutes.

Frank's pets often got him into scrapes. The worst case may have been when he was sharing a coach from Geisson to London with a stranger. He had with him a number of red slugs that he had collected in Germany. Awaking from a nap Buckland was horrified to see several of his slugs crawling slowly over the bald pate of his sleeping companion. Rather than try to explain the situation when the man awoke, he got out at the next stop.

Buckland died in December 1880, suffering from dropsy. His last words were, 'I think I shall see a great many curious animals.'

Buckland
William

Until he ate a bluebottle, William Buckland had always maintained that the taste of mole was the most repulsive he knew. Buckland, Oxford's first professor of geology and the father of Frank Buckland (q.v.), was remembered by Lord Playfair as 'a born experimentalist. I recollect various queer dishes which he had at his table. The hedgehog was a successful experiment. . . . I thought it good and tender. On another occasion I recollect a dish of crocodile, which was an utter failure.'

William Buckland was a remarkable man who among other things established geology as a respected subject of study in Britain and was the first person in England to recognise that glaciers had at one time covered much of Scotland and northern England.

In spite of all this undergroundology, as he referred to his science, Buckland seems to have had a boundless supply of energy for the performance of good works. He laid the first pipe drains in London; had Oxford lighted with gas; and lobbied for the use of coprolites (fossilised faeces) as fertilisers. As Canon of Christ Church, Buckland wrote the word GUANO in imported bird droppings on the turf in Tom's Quad. The extraordinary greenness of the letters as the summer wore on was an effective advertisement for his favourite fertiliser

When he went collecting, William usually rode a black mare

who was so well trained that whenever they passed a quarry she came to a halt and refused to move on until Buckland had dismounted and inspected the site. This automatic response became awkward when Buckland's only aim was to get to his destination as quickly as possible: if he rode the black mare he stopped at every quarry regardless.

His studies enabled him to develop remarkable detective skills. Riding towards London on a dark night, he and a friend found that they were lost. Dismounting and kneeling on the ground, Buckland scooped up a handful of earth, sniffed it, and pronounced 'Uxbridge'.

A more dramatic demonstration of his knowledge occurred on his honeymoon. William and his wife were taken to visit the shrine in Palermo of St Rosalia. The moment he saw her bones, preserved as relics, Buckland, to the horror of their hosts, exclaimed, 'Those are the bones of a goat – not of a woman!' Furious priests escorted the Bucklands out and immediately removed the bones from public view.

Long afterwards, on a visit to a foreign cathedral, William and his son, Frank, were shown a patch of floor marked with the blood of a martyr – stains which miraculously appeared fresh each day. With the aid of a memory and experience that few men could match, William dipped his fingers in the blood and, tasting it, said, 'I can tell you what it is; it is bat's urine!'

Edward Harcourt, Archbishop of York, and a great friend of William's, had been in Paris during the Revolution and purchased the heart of Louis XIV from someone who had plundered his tomb. He kept the embalmed heart in a snuff box and one day showed the curiosity to his friend. Commenting, 'I've eaten many things but never the heart of a king,' Buckland plucked it out of the box and swallowed it whole.

Lord Monboddo
Burnett
James

Lord Monboddo was a man of individual opinions, maintaining, among other things, that orangoutangs are a human species, capable of speech. He also believed that babies are born with tails but that there is a conspiracy of silence among midwives, who cut them off at birth. Monboddo was a careful observer at the births of his own children, but in each case the midwife outwitted him and managed to destroy the evidence.

According to the biographer Robert Chambers, Monboddo was 'by far the most learned judge . . . of his time'. Monboddo would not have found this a flattering comment, as he heartily despised 'his time': he had a passion for the ancients, their way of life and language. Though he was a just and compassionate landlord, Monboddo approved of slavery on the grounds that Plutarch had defended it. He also attempted to revive the religious beliefs of ancient Greece. Hearing of Dr Johnson's Dictionary, Monboddo expressed shock that a man of Johnson's ability could waste his time on English when Greek was clearly the only language worth preserving.

He lived quite simply, partly as a result of refusing to use any tool or convenience not enjoyed by the Greeks. In 1785, on one of his rare visits to London he was invited to observe a trial in progress at the Court of the King's Bench. The proceedings were interrupted when someone ran into the courtroom shouting that the roof was falling in. Panic ensued as lawyers, judges, and witnesses all ran to the door and tried to force their way out. Monboddo, who was deaf and short-sighted, sat through the entire episode quite calmly, making no attempt to join the fleeing masses. Finally, it was realised that the warning had been a false alarm and everyone returned to their seats. Asked how he had managed to remain so calm in the face of threatened disaster, Monboddo replied that he had supposed that he was watching an annual ceremony with which, as an alien to the English laws, he had no concern, but which he considered interesting to witness as a remnant of antiquity.

Capper
Joseph

apper, born of humble parents in Cheshire, made a small fortune as a grocer, and in 1779 decided to retire. He looked all over London for suitable lodgings, and at the end of one day's tedious search, found himself at the Horns, Konnington Capper's manner, even at the best of times, was surly and argumentative – indeed a contemporary once remarked that he 'never seemed so happy as when placed by the side of a churlish companion' – and when he called for supper and bed that night at the Horns, it was with his usual bad grace. The landlord took offence and refused, saying that no beds were available. Capper decided on the spot to stay there as long as was necessary to spite the landlord. Eventually the poor man capitulated and gave Capper a room which he kept until his death twenty-five years later. Every day he talked of moving out, refusing to make any long-term arrangements, though after some years he agreed to be billed by the fortnight.

Capper's way of life was very methodical. He had his favourite cup and refused to drink from any other. The same held true for his fork, knife, plate, etc. His meals never varied and neither did the pre-meal ritual of arranging his eating-things in a particular order, refusing to start until things were just so.

In the parlour each evening Capper sat alone while the other residents talked amongst themselves. It was his maxim to join in general conversation only when he had something ill-natured to say.

Something of a miser, Capper watched his investments with an eagle eye and had vowed never to lend to anyone. He had a soft side, though. When the landlord at the Horns asked him for a short-term loan, Capper replied, 'What is to be done, Mr Townsend? I have sworn not to lend.' With an anguished look he continued, 'I must therefore give it thee.'

He called himself 'The Champion of Government'. Any comments of an unpatriotic nature drew a furious response from him. The xenophobic haze through which he glowered at the world extended even to his hobby, which was killing flies.

With his cane raised over the intended victim, Capper invariably launched into a long story illustrating the perfidious nature of all Frenchmen, whom, he cried as he finished the deed, 'I hate and detest and would knock down just the same as this fly.'

Cavendish
Hon. Henry

Painfully shy and little known outside the Royal Society, Henry Cavendish was according to Humphrey Davy 'the most accomplished British philosopher of his time'. Among his many contributions to all branches of science was his demonstration of the composition of water.

Until 1783, when he was fifty-two, Cavendish lived with his father, who kept him on such a restricted allowance that the distinguished middle-aged scientist, heir to one of the greatest fortunes in England, came to Royal Society dinners with the cost of the meal, five shillings, in his pocket and not a penny more. Even after he inherited the Cavendish fortune, Henry took absolutely no interest in his wealth. One day when his banker called to inquire what Cavendish wished done with £80,000 of unspent income, the normally mild-mannered Cavendish lost his temper and threatened to change banks if he was to be continually interrupted about trivial matters.

He was equally indifferent to the pleasures of the table and at home always dined on leg of mutton. Once when he gave one of his very rare dinners for four scientist friends, the housekeeper, replying to the usual request for a leg of mutton said, 'Sir, that will not be enough for five.' 'Well, then,' he replied, 'get two!'

Communication with the servants was not usually verbal. Cavendish left notes to the housekeeper and developed an elaborate system of letter-boxes and double doors to ensure his privacy. After meeting a maid servant on the staircase, he had a second stairway built to spare himself any further upsetting encounters.

One of his few extravagances was a large private library which he kept in a house in Dean Street, Soho, under the care of a full-time librarian. Cavendish allowed his acquaintances to borrow books freely from his collection, but he himself never took a book without leaving a receipt.

His house in Clapham was given over to experimentation. The drawing room was kitted out as a laboratory; the next room housed a forge; the upper room served as an observatory; and he used one of the trees in the garden as a post for taking meteorological and astronomical readings.

Cavendish occasionally attended Sir Joseph Banks's scientific soirées and was remembered on one occasion standing for a long time on the threshold as if summoning up courage to face the crowd inside. When he finally entered he would shuffle from room to room, talking to himself in his high-pitched squeaky voice, hovering on the outskirts of conversations, and trying to avoid being approached.

At one of these gatherings he was accosted by a foreign gentleman who offered extravagant compliments and expressed his long-standing admiration. Cavendish, horribly ill at ease, stared at the floor and said nothing as the man went on. Suddenly he turned and fled from the room. He tore down the stairs, leapt into his waiting carriage, and was driven straight home. His startled admirer would have done better to heed Dr Woolaston's advice, 'The way to talk to Cavendish is never to look at him, but to talk as it were into a vacancy, and then it is not unlikely that you may set him going.'

Cavendish chose to die alone without the benefit of medical attention. He even sent his servant away, saying that he had something particular to think about and did not wish to be disturbed. After his death he was discovered to be the largest holder of Bank-stock in England; he left £1,175,000 to his cousin, Lord George Cavendish who, as his heir, had been suffered by Cavendish to pay him an annual visit of half an hour for some years past.

Lord Brougham, who knew Henry Cavendish, said 'He probably uttered fewer words in the course of his life than any man who lived to fourscore years, not at all excepting the monks at La Trappe.'

Champion
Sir Claude

The perfect 'Boy's Own Paper' hero, Sir Claude Champion de Crespigny believed that 'where there is a daring deed to be done in any part of the world, an Englishman should leap to the front to accomplish it.' Though Sir Claude had a long and adventurous career, many of his attempts to leap to the front were thwarted by bureaucrats opposed to his breakneck schemes. In 1886 Stanley turned down his request to accompany the Livingstone expedition on the grounds that Sir Claude had not got enough experience of Central Africa. This was disappointing, but, in his own words, 'even more keenly have I had cause to regret my lot in not being able to take part as a volunteer in several of our little African wars.'

Three years later, when he was forty-two, Sir Claude went on his own to Egypt where there was a Dervish uprising, but, in spite of his claim to be war correspondent for the *Sporting Times*, he was refused permission to go to the front. He tried to get over this disappointment by volunteering for the Boer War. Earlier he had failed to persuade Blondin, the man who crossed Niagara Falls on a tightrope, to let him take a turn on the high wire. On a trip to Havana, Sir Claude had to be forcibly stopped from leaping into the bullring and trying his luck.

Following family tradition, Sir Claude pursued a military career. He joined the navy at thirteen and five years later transferred to the King's Royal Rifle Corps. He was stationed in Ireland, took up steeplechasing and earned the nickname, 'The Mad Rider'. Later he was sent to India where he was introduced to the joys of big-game hunting. He was also an excellent swimmer and sailed competitively. In 1883 Sir Claude and a partner became the first people to cross the North Sea in a balloon.

Although he had broken fourteen bones before middle age, Sir Claude did not slow down much as the years passed. At forty-two he became the first European to swim the Nile rapids. When he was sixty-one he walked the 45 miles from Champion Lodge in Essex to London on a wager of 2s 6d. He steeplechased until he was sixty-seven. In 1920, at the age of seventy-three he challenged his cousin to a duel and was sorely grieved that his challenge was rejected.

Sir Claude's hair-raising adventures were not expressions of a morbid death-wish. He loved his family and very much enjoyed life. His wife was also made of stern stuff and their two sons survived a vigorous upbringing – learning to swim, for instance, when their father pushed them overboard while sailing on the Blackwater – to become distinguished soldiers and keen sportsmen.

Sir Claude believed that fighting was a manly occupation and an indication of character. His obituary in *The Times* notes that 'as a man of honour, he regretted the passing of the duel as the proper means of obtaining satisfaction.' Men who applied to work at Champion Lodge had first to box with their putative employer. Only those who showed spirit were considered. If he came across a tramp, who looked reasonably fit, Sir Claude would invite him to box for a meal. His friends once dressed a professional boxer in rags and stationed him in Sir Claude's path. The inevitable challenge was given and accepted, and Sir Claude was duly trounced. He enjoyed the joke, and continued to issue his challenges.

Christie
John

John Christie, the rich and enterprising founder of the Glyndebourne Festival Opera, was not above using his distinguished position to indulge a schoolboy sense of fun. Sitting next to the Queen at dinner one evening, he removed his glass eye and polished it for several minutes with his handkerchief. When he had finished, he popped it back, turned to the Queen and asked 'In straight, Ma'am?' He enjoyed introducing people by the wrong names, and took a great delight in simply being provocative; for a time all female guests to Glyndebourne were provided with knitting needles and wool. It is perhaps not surprising to learn that he spent sixteen years as a master at Eton. He loved it, particularly the food, and had been known to eat seven helpings of tapioca pudding at a sitting. Years later when he built a restaurant in connection with one of his business ventures he made sure that milk pudding was on the menu every day. His experience as a schoolmaster also served him well in the trenches during the First World War, where he entertained his men with readings from Spenser's *Faerie Queene*, Plato's *Dialogues* and *Alice through the Looking Glass*, with a question period at the end of each session.

Christie was something of a dandy, but certainly not a slave to fashion. At one time he owned 180 handkerchiefs, 132 pairs of socks, and 110 shirts; yet he often wore a pair of old tennis shoes with formal evening dress. For a time lederhosen were practically a uniform with him and in the summer of 1933 all visitors to Glyndebourne were expected to wear lederhosen or dirndls.

Christie never felt the cold, so, unless there was a guests' revolt, Glyndebourne was heated in winter by one small electric fire with a long cord that was trailed from room to room. He always travelled third class and never tipped a waiter, instead making a point of politely explaining to the disappointed attendant that tips were an insult to the recipient.

Along with his small parsimonies, Christie was capable of the grand gesture. He bought the Empress Josephine's diamonds – a tiara, necklace and brooch – to celebrate the imminent birth of his first child and took the opportunity to test his theory that a brown paper parcel wrapped with string would never attract the attention of a thief. He wrapped up the diamonds, left them on his third-class railway seat, and went to buy a paper. When he returned, the parcel was still there.

Buying in bulk was a habit of Christie's. He once found himself in possession of 2000 pairs of plastic dancing pumps. As the market for plastic pumps was sluggish at that time, he tried to unload them on members of his club, Brooks's. As Wilfred Blunt tells the story, Brooks's was littered for months with unwanted plastic dancing pumps.

Christie was devoted to dogs; he had planned to build kennels and a dog-cafeteria for the pets of visitors to the Opera, but the project was never completed. His favourite pug, George, is buried at Glyndebourne in a grave marked by a little headstone and protected by iron railings.

'Romeo Coates'
Coates
Robert

Robert Coates was a sensational success on the stage for a number of years on account of his unbelievably bad acting. The *New Monthly Magazine* said in 1872, 'Never shall I forget his representation of Lothario some sixty years since, at the Haymarket Theatre, for his own pleasure, as he accurately termed it.'

Coates broke new ground, not only in his interpretation of his two major parts, Romeo and Lothario, but also in his conception of the costumes appropriate to those roles. A blue silk cloak covered with spangles, a Charles II wig and a top hat seemed right for Romeo, while as Lothario, a more modern figure,

Coates appeared in a silver suit, a pink silk stole, a gold sword and a large hat with ostrich-feather plumes.

In Antigua, where Coates was born, he had made a speciality of Romeo, always travelling with his costume for the role. Known as 'Romeo Coates', he continued in his devotion to the Bard when he settled in Bath. A fellow-resident at Coates's boarding house, overhearing him misquote a passage from *Romeo and Juliet*, reminded him of the correct wording. 'Aye,' he replied, 'that is the reading, I know, for I have the whole play by heart, but I think I have improved on it.'

Perhaps Coates's greatest contribution to dramatic art was his lack of inhibition about communicating directly with the audience. As an amateur, he insisted, he had a right to enjoy himself, and not to be bound by petty conventions of the theatre – such as that which forbade his waving to his friends during a performance. When, as frequently happened, Coates's appearance on stage was greeted with crowing and catcalls, he interrupted the play to reprimand the rowdies in the audience. On one occasion he drew his sword on them.

According to some critics, Coates's highest achievement was his interpretation of the death scene in *Romeo and Juliet*. Holding himself in such a way as to display to the greatest advantage his bejewelled costume and the symmetry of his bowed legs, he prepared to die. First he swept the stage with a silk handkerchief. Then he removed his hat and set it carefully upon the floor. Finally he laid himself down, tossing and turning until he found a comfortable position. Audiences, overcome with emotion at this sight, often demanded one or even two encores and they were seldom disappointed.

Contemporary reports describe Coates as having an inflexibility of limb, an awkwardness of gait and an idiotic manner of standing still which evoked hysteria even before he opened his mouth to speak. This physical ungainliness, combined with a total misunderstanding of every passage he spoke, a tendency to forget lines and then to debate with himself on stage as to the appropriate wording, and a habit of mispronunciation, help to explain his brief but spectacular success.

In Bath and later in London Coates made a great impression in public. His carriage, pulled by two beautifully matched white horses, was in the shape of a huge cockle shell, with a step in the form of a rooster. This was a reference to Coates's emblem, a cock, and his motto, 'While I live, I'll crow', both of which decorated all things Coatesian, including the silver buttons on his servants' livery. Later the cockle-shell carriage was replaced by another which looked like a kettledrum and was hung upon two large serpents. These equipages gave him the nicknames 'Curricle Coates' and 'Cock-a-doodle-Coates'.

He was also called 'Diamond Coates' for the masses of diamonds he wore on stage and off. These he was much attached to and during one performance of *Romeo and Juliet* in 1811, he caused the audience to dissolve into hysterics when he refused to quit the stage at an exit line because he was hunting for a diamond shoe-buckle that had fallen off during that scene. Coates himself preferred the sobriquet, 'The Celebrated Philanthropic Amateur', for most of his performances were charity benefits.

Coates also wrote poetry and addressed some of his best verses to Miss Tylney Long, a society beauty, whom he hoped to marry. Alas, his appeals fell on deaf ears: she was impervious to the refined sentiment expressed in such lines as, 'Give me your hand – your cash let others take.'

Cope
Henry

Most Brighton residents knew the Green Man, by sight at least. It was difficult not to notice him as he promenaded on The Steine, wearing green pantaloons, green waistcoat, green frock coat, green cravat, green gloves, and carrying a green-silk handkerchief and a watch with green seals. His face itself, with powdered ears, whiskers, eyebrows and chin, was green just from the reflections. He travelled in a green carriage, attended by a green-liveried groom holding a green whip. The Green Man's real name was Henry Cope. He was the son of a 'good family', as was indicated by his gentlemanly manner and the financial resources which enabled him to support himself in the colour to which he was accustomed.

He lived in a room which was painted green and filled with green sofas, chairs, tables and curtains. His bedclothes, too, were green and he ate only green fruits and vegetables. The poor Green Man came to a sad end one day in 1806 when he was walking by the sea. Reaching the edge of a cliff, he just kept walking and fell to his death.

Curtis
James

Mr Curtis was besotted with the Old Bailey and the business conducted therein. For over twenty-five years he was in daily attendance there, taking down verbatim the testimony of every case heard in the New Court – the Old Court he, for some reason, despised and refused ever to set foot in. His court reporting was strictly for his own amusement, though he was by no means a wealthy man. He did, however, develop a system which enabled him accurately to record hours of spoken evidence and this system he imparted to the public under the title *Shorthand Made Shorter*.

Only a public execution could induce Curtis to miss a day at Court. Having faithfully followed the progress of a trial, he did not lose interest after the sentencing, but made it a point to witness the punishment. He befriended many of the convicted and kept them company during their last days.

Curtis's devotion to his hobby was extraordinary. He walked 29 miles before breakfast to attend the execution of Captain Moir at Chelmsford. He became friends with Corder, the murderer of Maria Marten, stood with him in the dock, and eventually wrote his biography. Their close relationship led an artist from a provincial paper, who had been sent to Corder's trial to take a sketch of the accused, to mistake Curtis for the guilty man. Curtis's picture duly appeared on the front page over the name of the notorious Corder. Far from being outraged, Curtis delighted in telling this story on himself. Indeed, he appeared in some way to be flattered by it.

For some inexplicable reason the mild-mannered Curtis was continually mistaken for more sinister persons. On his only visit to Dover he was arrested as a French spy, and when he went to Captain Moir's execution he was almost turned out of his room because the landlady took it into her head that he was to be the executioner.

Actually, as James Grant, editor of the *Morning Herald* and a friend of Curtis, describes him, Curtis was honest, kind-hearted, and inoffensive. He was also extremely hardy. In 1834, just for fun, Curtis did without a proper night's sleep for 100 days, dozing occasionally for an hour or two in an armchair and otherwise going about his normal activities.

Besides frequenting the Old Bailey, Curtis's great amusement was walking, ideally in the rain. He was never seen in a vehicle of any kind. Up by 4.00 a.m. – 'it was an event in his life to lie in bed till five', Grant tells us – by seven he had walked 6 or 8 miles. Retracing his steps was a positive joy to Curtis; he usually managed to go over the same ground two or three times in a morning before appearing at the Old Bailey. To be asked by an acquaintance to walk 10 or 12 miles on an errand was, he felt, the greatest possible kindness. He frequently inquired of his friends whether they had any business in the outlying villages of London, adding, in the case of an affirmative answer, that he would be happy to 'take a step' with them.

'The Twig of the Garden'
Cussans
William

William Cussans was financially independent – he was rumoured to be the illegitimate son of Nathaniel Curzon, Baron Scarsdale (1726–1804) – and could have lived a comfortable life had he chosen to do so. Instead he became a familiar character in and around Covent Garden where he worked at odd jobs on whims or wagers and became known as 'the Twig of the Garden'. He was once challenged to spend three months as a waiter at the Red Lion pub without ever losing his temper. He won the bet and gave his winnings to his fellow waiters. For six months he was, as a contemporary observer put it, 'in a silent mood' and refused to speak to anyone. He did not become a recluse, however. Instead he communicated with friends by means of a slate which he carried with him everywhere.

His costume varied, but he was often seen wearing an enormous cocked hat on his shaved head, paper ruffles at his throat and wrists, a heavy chain around his neck, and a sword at his side. Once Cussans gave a tailor precise instructions for a new outfit: 'Cut the skirts of my coat into strips and sew them on my waistcoat, breeches and stockings.'

He wrote comic verse. One of his creations, 'Oh Poor Robinson Crusoe' was sung by him at Sadler's Wells and the Royal Circus 'to universal applause':

He got all the wood
That ever he could '
　　And he stuck it together with glue, so.
He made him a hut
And in it he put
　　The carcase of Robinson Crusoe.

Walking in Temple Gardens one evening, Cussans asked three ladies who were passing whether they had ever seen a man swim. 'No,' said one, 'nor do we wish to see such a sight.' 'But you shall', he giggled, and jumped fully clothed into the Thames. In spite of their professed desire not to witness such a spectacle, the ladies were rooted to the spot. After swimming around for a while, the object of their astonishment climbed out, bowed elegantly to them, and walked off, leaving them in no doubt that they had encountered 'the eccentric Mr Cussans'.

The patrons of a Bath coffee-shop were even more amazed one very cold day to see Cussans, wearing a bright yellow suit, sit down, call for a pitcher of water and pour it over himself. He then ordered a large meal, a newspaper, a bootjack, the Bible, a pint of vinegar, a paper of pins, and some barley sugar. When the landlord failed to deliver these items, Cussans took six shirts out of his suitcase, and put them on over his other clothes and then 'very coolly' directed that a dish of cold fried milestones, without sugar, be ready for him in the evening and that his bed be sprinkled with sawdust. Finally, he rose, bowed to the company with great dignity and left.

Dancer
Daniel

ancer was the son of one miser and grandson of another. His two brothers and one sister all shared his parsimonious tendencies, but in terms of tightfistedness Daniel was the undisputed leader. Before his father's death, Dancer had shown no particular signs of avarice, but he changed almost at once. Although he believed that his father had hidden £1,500 somewhere about the farm, he preferred to leave the money undiscovered rather than risk alerting his brothers to its existence and being obliged to share it with them.

As the eldest son, Daniel inherited a farm and 80 acres of rich land at Harrow Weald in Middlesex, but he balked at the expense of cultivating it, so the land lay fallow. He lived not in the main house but in a run-down shack elsewhere on the property, with his sister as housekeeper. Every Saturday she cooked one piece of beef and fourteen hard dumplings, which were made to last for the whole week.

When luck was with them, the Dancers could avoid even this small expense. On one of their walks, Daniel and his sister were fortunate enough to come across a rotting sheep that had died of some disease. This they dragged home, skinned, and made into mutton pies which they hoarded as great delicacies. When a neighbour at this time remarked that Miss Dancer looked a bit downcast, she explained that her brother had accused her of extravagance in going through the mutton pies too quickly.

Miss Dancer was seldom seen outside the house, but Daniel liked to wander, collecting bones to gnaw, and cow dung with which he built a hiding-place for his money. According to one biographer, he was so mean that 'when he was obliged to relieve the wants of nature, he would rather walk two miles than not assist in manuring his own land.'

In 1766 his sister died. Dancer had refused all suggestions that a doctor should be called on the grounds that 'if the old girl's time is come, the nostrums of all the quacks in Christendom cannot save her – she may as well die now as at any future time.' Miss Dancer's place was taken by a servant named Griffiths, a like-minded soul who had managed, before he joined Dancer, to save £500 out of wages which never came to more than £10 a year.

A neighbour, Lady Tempest, solicitous for Dancer's health, prevailed upon him to buy a hat for one shilling. The next time she saw him he was bare-headed. When she expressed surprise, Dancer explained that he had sold the hat to Griffiths for a sixpence profit. On another occasion Lady Tempest sent Dancer a dish of trout stewed in claret. He loved trout, but this gift presented him with a terrible dilemma: the expense of lighting a fire to heat it was too horrible to contemplate; on the other hand, cold foods were liable to give him toothache. He solved the problem simply by sitting on the trout until it was warm enough to eat safely.

Dancer considered washing with soap and towels a waste of money. He would wait for a sunny day, scrub himself with sand at a nearby pond, and lie in the sun to dry. His cleanliness regimen caused Cyrus Redding, a nineteenth-century writer, to comment, that, 'notwithstanding his solitary tendencies as a miser . . . he was never without a colony of insect friends attached to his person.'

Although Dancer didn't take snuff, he begged a pinch whenever he could. Once a month or so, when his snuff box was full, he took it to a candle-maker and exchanged it for a farthing candle which was made to last until the box was replenished.

As might be expected, he was plagued with robbers attracted by rumours of piles of gold lying about his rotting house, but he hid his money well and they seldom got away with much. On one occasion a pack of burglars had to hang Dancer by the neck several times before he agreed to lead the way to a small portion of his hidden treasure. After this he decided to take precautions to secure his house.

Like a number of misers, Dancer was stricter with himself than with others. Griffiths, his servant, ate whatever he wanted and slept on a comfortable bed. A neighbour offered to accompany Dancer to Aylesbury on some business. When, after a day's riding (Dancer as usual on a sack instead of a saddle) they reached an inn, Daniel said to his companion, 'Pray, Sir, do you go into the house, order what you please and live like a gentleman, I will settle for it readily; but as for myself, I must go on in my old way.' He bought a pennysworth of bread; slept under his horse's manger; and the next morning cheerfully paid his friend's bill of £15.00.

Day
Thomas

Thomas Day was a romantic idealist, a disciple of Rousseau, who expressed his contempt for the artificialties of the modern world by going barefoot, wearing long hair, dressing simply and speaking bluntly. He was also high-principled and generous – from his schooldays he gave away most of his money and possessions to the poor. So tender-hearted was he that when called upon by a lawyer friend to kill a spider he refused, saying, 'I don't know that I have a right. Suppose that a superior being said to a companion, 'Kill that lawyer', how should you like it? And a lawyer is more noxious to most people than a spider.'

Although he had fulfilled the requirements, Day left Oxford without a degree because he didn't believe in titles or distinctions. He wanted to live in the country and work to improve the life of farm workers, but he did not want to live alone. He knew that only an extraordinary woman would be willing and able to share his spartan existence, and he decided that the surest way to find such a paragon would be to raise and train her himself.

Accordingly, in 1769, with the help of a lawyer, James Bicknell, Day adopted two twelve-year-old orphans – a blonde named Lucretia and a brunette named Sabrina. There were strict conditions attached to the adoption to ensure that the girls' honour was protected and Day promised to make fair provision for whichever did not become his wife.

His first step was to remove them from all corrupting influences. He took them both to live with him alone at Avignon beyond the sound of spoken English, and started their instruction in literature, science and moral philosophy. After a year, however, the problems presented by two squabbling adolescent girls induced Day to bring them back to London, where Lucretia, who had turned out to be invincibly stupid, was apprenticed to a milliner. Day continued to maintain her until her marriage some years later.

Sabrina and he removed to Lichfield to continue her education, but she was not overfond of books and failed to live up to his exacting standards of physical and moral courage. According to one of his neighbours, Anna Seward, Day was disappointed at Sabrina's faint-heartedness; when he dropped melted sealing-wax upon her arms she did not endure it heroically, nor when he fired at her petticoats pistols, which she believed to be charged with balls, could she help starting aside, or suppress her screams.

In any case, Sabrina was growing too old to be without a female companion, and was therefore sent to a boarding school, where she stayed until she was seventeen. She later married Bicknell, the lawyer who had helped Day adopt her, and, after his early death, became housekeeper to Samuel Johnson's friend, Dr Burney.

Leaving behind his experiments in wife-moulding, Day fell in love with another neighbour in Lichfield, Miss Honora Sneyd. When she rejected him, he transferred his attentions to her younger sister, Elizabeth. Elizabeth explained to Day that his rough manners and appearance were not calculated to win the heart of well brought-up young ladies. Although his neglect of conventions of dress and behaviour had been based on principle, Day resolved to change himself for the sake of love. He went to France for a year where he studied dancing and fencing and stood daily for an hour or more in a wooden frame in an effort to straighten his legs and improve his posture. He did not abandon his charitable activities during this time: there is a story that he gave so much to the poor of Lyons that on his departure they sent a message asking him to leave enough money to tide them over until he returned.

Upon his return to England, Day offered himself again to Elizabeth. Once again, she turned him down, this time on the grounds that the visible effort which accompanied his social performances made him more ridiculous than his previous unfashionable, but natural behaviour.

Thus rejected, Day moved to London where he attempted to forget women and occupied himself writing pamphlets supporting the abolition of slave trade and higher wages for farm labourers. The Sneyd sisters, perpetuating their curious habit of handing down lovers, both married Day's friend R L Edgeworth – first, Honora and in 1780, after her sister's death, Elizabeth.

While in London, Day became acquainted with Miss Esther Milnes, a wealthy and intelligent woman who shared his ideals. He was naturally shy of being hurt, but she loved him and after a long friendship they married in 1778. Day insisted, however, that Esther retain complete control over her own fortune in case she should ever tire of the harsh regimen he proposed.

They moved to a small farm in Essex to put his theories into practice. The soil was poor and the farm consistently lost money, but the workers were well treated. Mrs Day was allowed no servants, no singing or dancing. Even her beloved harpsichord was off-bounds. 'We have no right to luxuries while the poor want bread', was Day's reasoning. They worked hard – so much so that Day could not take time to instruct the house-builder where to put the bedroom windows, and the room was completed as a windowless cell. After three years the clay soil defeated them and the Days moved to a farm at Ottershaw, Surrey. Here they continued their work, eventually giving away almost all they owned.

Day died as a result of his principles. He objected to breaking in horses, believing that they would respond to kindness alone. One day when riding an unbroken colt on a visit to his mother, he was thrown on his head at Wargrave and died from his injuries. Esther Day was broken-hearted and took to her bed. For two years, until her death in 1791, she lived in darkness, rising only at night. She is buried at Wargrave, beside her husband.

Densham
F. W.

Church attendance at Warleggan, Cornwall, fell dramatically while the Rev. F W Densham was rector there. He contrived to quarrel with almost all his parishioners, losing most of them when he painted their twelfth-century church red and blue, with black- and white-striped pillars, traces of which decor still remain. Although in his last year as rector, only one person attended Sunday service – and that on only one occasion – the church was never empty. Each vacant seat was occupied by a cardboard cut-out or name card supplied by Father Densham to replace his dwindling congregation.

Father Densham never visited his parishioners or ventured into the village. Instead he set up an eight-foot barbed-wire fence around the rectory with a box for mail and provisions. He consented to see people by appointment only, and if they were even one minute late they would find the door locked. Until his death in 1953, Father Densham lived mainly on porridge and nettles, and chose to have no furniture at all in the rectory. The garden, however, was full of little games and roundabouts he had constructed for children. None ever came.

Dering
George Edward

George Edward Dering, the squire of Lockeleys, Welwyn, was known locally as 'the tight-rope-walking inventor'. His inventions, mostly railway and electrical devices, earned him a fellowship in the Royal Society; his interest in high-wire stunts brought him the friendship of the greatest practitioner of that art, Blondin. In the late 1850s, shortly before Blondin made his sensational crossing of Niagara Falls, Dering and he rehearsed together on a rope stretched across the River Mimram, near Lockeley. Blondin, blindfolded, pushed Dering across in a wheelbarrow or carried him in a sack.

For the most part, Dering lived quietly. He entertained seldom and spent most of his time reading. A local book-seller had a standing order from Dering for every book published – in any language – about electricity. Eventually this influx got the better of him and there were piles of unopened parcels of books around the house.

Dering needed peace for his work and he went to some lengths to obtain it. The shutters were closed all day to keep out noise. Any farmer whose sheep grazed Dering's land was asked to remove all new-born lambs from the park lest their bleatings disturb him. Dering lived largely at night when distractions were fewer and dined at two o'clock in the morning. He bought the house next door to his in Brighton, lock, stock and barrel, rather than put up with the neighbour's barking dog. Back at Lockeleys, Dering spent £20,000 building a new public highway entirely at his own expense to divert the noisy traffic from an existing road that ran too near his house.

Before his passion for silence became overwhelming, Dering kept Lockeleys well-stocked with game and every year invited one of the neighbouring farmers to come and shoot. Though they were not allowed into the house, offered any hospitality, or asked to meet their host, the farmers were free to bag as many pheasant, quail or guinea fowl as they could. But they were absolutely forbidden to harm the pigeons.

For a period of about thirty years prior to 1907 Dering became an absentee landlord. No one knew where he spent his time, or when he would return to Lockeleys. The staff of seven kept everything in readiness for an unexpected visit; Dering left a standing order for a mutton chop to be ready whenever he arrived. Ordinarily he came only once a year, just before Christmas. He settled accounts, paid wages, looked at a twelve-month's accumulation of unopened post and always left on Christmas morning.

In 1907 Dering once again took up residence at Lockeleys, but now he lived in only one room into which no one else dared venture. His love of solitude had grown with the years and eventually he dismissed all his servants and staff, sold his sheep and cattle, and let the estate run wild. Only after his death was the full extent of Dering's need for silence revealed. To their astonishment his friends and neighbours learned that he had for many years been living in Brighton under the name of Dale with a wife and a child. Dering's daughter was even more surprised to find herself heir to Lockeleys and an impressive fortune, neither of which had been known to her during her father's lifetime.

Digweed
Ernest

Ernest Digweed, a retired schoolmaster from Portsmouth, who died in 1976, left £26,000 in the care of the Public Trustee with the following instructions: 'If during these 80 years, the Lord Jesus Christ shall come to reign on earth, then the Public Trustee upon obtaining proof which shall satisfy them of His identity shall pay to the Lord Jesus Christ all the property which they hold on his behalf.' If by 2056 the Lord has not appeared to claim the bequest the whole amount will revert to the State.

Dinely-Goodere
Sir John

Sir John's primary object in life was the retrieval of £300,000 which he believed, on no very good authority, could be his for the relatively small expense of a lawsuit. By 1770 his position had become desperate. He was forced to sell what was left of the family estate at Burhope in Herefordshire, and decided to get the money he needed to pursue his claim through the courts by marrying a rich woman.

Friends had managed to procure him a pension as a poor knight of Windsor, and it was from the illustrious address of Windsor Castle that he began his campaign. The ancient and honourable name of Dinely was worth, he reckoned, a dowry of at least £10,000. But should the lucky woman he chose to marry be young and pretty he might lower his price by £500. He studied the market closely and made a list of eligible women, with notes on their fortunes, faces and figures.

He lived very simply while at Windsor, saving what money he had for his thrice-yearly visits to London. These he announced by means of advertisements placed in the fashionable papers, replies 'to be left at the Admiralty coffee-house till called for, post-paid or your letter will not be received.' His reputation spread, and it was not long before Sir John was surrounded by women whenever he appeared at the theatre or at Vauxhall

Gardens, his two favourite haunts. Dressed in faded velvet breeches, a coat and waistcoat of a cut popular years before, and a powdered wig which was secured to his head by means of a chin strap, he cut a conspicuous, if not a dashing, figure.

As soon as he spied a likely candidate for matrimony, Sir John would approach her, bow deeply, and without a word present her with a piece of paper from a stock which he carried with him, setting forth the terms of his romantic proposition. His search for a wife continued without success until his death at the age of sixty-nine. More than once he discovered that the object of his affections was a man in disguise, but neither practical jokes nor his years of failure discouraged him from continuing his search. One of his advertisements is reproduced below.

To the angelic fair of the true English breed: – worthy notice. Sir John Dinely, of Windsor Castle, recommends himself and his ample fortune to any angelic beauty of good breed, fit to become, and willing to be, a mother of a noble heir, and keep up the name of an ancient family, ennobled by deeds of arms and ancestral renown. Ladies at a certain period of life need not apply, as heirship is the object of the mutual contract offered by the ladies' sincere admirer, Sir John Dinely. Fortune favours the bold. Such ladies as this advertisement may induce to apply, or send their agents (but not servants or matrons) may direct to me at the Castle, Windsor. Happiness and pleasure are agreeable objects, and should be regarded as well as honour. The lady who shall thus become my wife will be a Baronetess, and rank accordingly as Lady Dinely, of Windsor. Goodwill and favour to all ladies of Great Britain; pull no caps on his account, but favour him with your smiles, and paeans of pleasure await your steps.
Ipswich Journal, *21 August 1802*

Douglas
Alexander Hamilton

The 10th Duke of Hamilton, often called the proudest man in Britain, combined in one person three dukes, two marquises, three earls and eight barons. He was the premier peer in Scotland and could trace his family at least as far as the thirteenth century. Above all, he insisted that he was the true heir to the throne of Scotland. This claim was based on his conviction that James VI had been secretly killed as a baby and an imposter substituted. The crown therefore should have descended through the heir-apparent, a Douglas, to the 10th Duke.

Visitors to the Duke's home on Arran profited from his lordship's feudal view of the world. Like a medieval ruler he threw his regal cloak of protection over those fortunate enough to enter his domain. All guests were given a token which entitled them to lodge, board and travel anywhere on the island entirely at the Duke's expense. Not infrequently visitors took advantage of this arrangement to stay rather longer on Arran then they had originally planned, and in fact, a number became resident there for the lifetime of the Duke.

He showed a democratic streak, however, in choosing a wife. He married a commoner, Miss Susan Beckford, daughter of William Beckford of Fonthill (q.v.) and one of the great beauties of her day. Though not of royal blood, she was the grand-daughter of a Hamilton, which, apparently, counted for a lot. In any case, as the Duke's obituary in *The Times* in 1852 pointed out, 'he could not expect to find a Princess worthy of his hand.'

Hamilton Palace was the family seat, and it was there that the Duke intended to be buried. He outbid the British Museum for a magnificent sarcophagus that had been made for an Egyptian princess. When the tomb, for which Hamilton paid £11,000, arrived at Hamilton Palace it became all too clear that Egyptian princesses were substantially shorter than Scottish Dukes. Attempts to lengthen the tomb were unsuccessful due to the unusually hard nature of the stone from which it was made. The Duke suffered great anxiety over this and often lay down in the sarcophagus to try to assure himself that he would fit.

He decided to build a mausoleum that would be a worthy

receptacle for his sarcophagus and serve as the final resting-place for all the Dukes of Hamilton, past and future. Described by Timbs as 'the most costly and magnificent temple for the reception of the dead in the world – always excepting the pyramids', the Hamilton Mausoleum was a domed structure 120 feet high. The floor was marble inlaid with other rare stones; the doors were replicas of those carved by Ghiberti for the Baptistry in Florence; inside there was an octagonal chapel, numerous statues, the tombs of the first nine Dukes, the great sarcophagus of the 10th Duke and room for future generations. The splendour was not lost on Hamilton. 'What a grand sight it will be', he used to say, 'when twelve Dukes of Hamilton rise together here at the Resurrection.'

Like the Pharaohs of Egypt, he chose to be embalmed and his last journey was to purchase the embalming spices. On his death bed fears that the sarcophagus would be too small returned and his last words were, 'Double me up! Double me up!' Hamilton's fears were justified; his feet had to be cut off and placed in the tomb separately. Perhaps it is best that he was spared the last blow to his pride: the later discovery that the sarcophagus which housed his remains had held the body, not of a princess, but of the court jester.

Duchess of Queensberry
Douglas
Catherine

Catherine Hyde, the Duchess of Queensberry, was a beautiful and strong-willed woman who took little notice of the opinions of others. She was banned from Court for soliciting George III for a donation to have Gay's political satire, *Polly*, printed after the King himself had forbidden its public performance. Before this episode, while she was still more or less in the King's good graces, a Royal Order on dress had to be passed to prevent Catherine from appearing at Court dressed in red flannel and wearing a maid's apron. She thought elaborate clothes a waste of time and effort; rather than spend hours before a party having her hair dressed and powdered, she would set out for her destina-

tion on foot, often walking several miles and turning up cheerful, sweaty, and red-faced with exertion.

She was a celebrated literary and political hostess and her
parties offered scope for a free expression of her quirks.
Catherine was tyrannical about times of arrival and departure –
late arrivals were turned away and when she tired of her guests
she used to pick up a broom and begin sweeping the floor
energetically, a signal, as regular guests knew, that they had
better go soon. To the Duchess of Bedford, who had been difficult over some social arrangement, Catherine sent this note:

> 'Come with a whistle and come with a call;
> Come with a good will or come not at all.'

One poor girl in whose honour the Duchess had promised to give
a party found that when the invitations where issued she was not
even included among the guests. The girl's father, the Duke of
Bridgewater, wrote to the Duchess to point out the omission and
received this reply: 'The advertisement came to hand: it was very
pretty and ingenious, but everything that is pretty and ingenious
does not always succeed . . . postponed but not forgot;
unalterable! Adieu!'

At another party, George Selwyn, Horace Walpole, and Lord
Lorn were huddled together in a quiet room with a fire, as much
for warmth as for conversation. The Duchess came into the room
and withdrew immediately without a word. Soon after a servant
arrived and began removing the door from its hinges. The three
gentlemen took the hint and returned to the ballroom.

Catherine's friends, among whom were Pope, Pitt, Congreve,
and Swift, loved her for her wit, her beauty and her freedom of
spirit; but they had to learn to live with her impulsive behaviour.
She once arrived at a friend's house in Parson's Green, having
driven down from London in a mad hurry to deliver some urgent
news. 'What is it?' asked her worried friend. 'Take a couple of
beefsteaks, clap them together as if they were a dumpling, and
eat them with pepper and salt; it is the best thing you ever tasted.
I couldn't help coming to tell you this,' she said, settling back in
her carriage for the journey home.

Duff
Jamie

Jamie Duff was a character of the Edinburgh streets who gained early notoriety when he entered himself as a runner in the Leith horse-races. He ran the course barefoot, half bent over, whipping himself with a switch and behaving in every way like a horse with a rider.

He acquired the nickname Bailie Duff when he later elected to take up a more dignified way of life. In imitation of a bailie, he adopted a brass chain, a cocked hat, and a wig. Most people humoured Duff in this harmless whim but there was one bailie who objected to the imposture and ordered Duff to remove his badges of office. As Duff was a popular character, the official's petty abuse of power soon became the butt of public satires, in prose, poetry and pictures.

In any case Jamie found that ceremonial garb, and the role that went with it, suited him and he devoted himself henceforth to attending funerals where his air of solemn dignity could be appreciated. He went to almost every funeral in Edinburgh for upwards of forty years, always leading the procession and dressed in his own mourning costume – weepers, a black cravat, crape, and a black hat which he dyed deeper black for special funerals such as that in 1776 of David Hume, the philosopher. Though he was never formally engaged to accompany a funeral procession, Duff became such a fixture that he was more or less expected to appear and a payment of ½ shilling for his services was customary.

Apart from his mourning costume Jamie was not usually a well-dressed figure. His stockings hung loose about his ankles; he shuffled along and couldn't speak distinctly except while swearing, when his voice became wonderfully clear. He was occasionally teased by small boys who sent him after non-existent funerals, and when he was so provoked, Jamie had a worrying tendency to lash out at the first person he might see, no matter how innocent. However, no great damage was done this way as he was not really a violent man.

He was very anxious to stay out of the army, which at a certain period was bribing people to join by offering silver coins. So worried was Jamie by the prospect of being tricked into joining that he decided to refuse all offers of money, lest the

71

donor turn out to be a recruiting officer. Since his income consisted largely of donations from the citizens of Edinburgh, this policy caused him real hardship and distressed his many friends. Finally, Duff's mother prevailed upon him to take his nephew, who was too young for the army, on his strolls about the city to accept coins on his behalf. This arrangement satisfied everyone.

Jamie lived with his mother and was very conscientious about her. He always dined with her and if invited by friends to share a meal, Jamie merely sat with them as they ate and afterwards put his portion, including soups and sauces, into his pocket (which was definitely not waterproof) and took it back to his mother. Chambers tells us that 'it was his custom to throw all his greetings into her lap, and he has been known to offend her highly by defiling her apron with bloody sheep-heads, garbage, etc., or sousing her with pail-fuls of nasty, though nutritious fluids.'

Egerton
Francis Henry

gerton, the 8th Earl of Bridgewater, spent most of his life as the Rev. Mr Egerton, but his interests were more academic than spiritual and his career in the church owed much to the influence of his father, the Bishop of Durham. In 1796 he left England for France, possibly to avoid scandal about one or more illegitimate children, but also partly for the sake of his health. He quarrelled with his brother, eventually the 7th Earl, and he was disappointed in the legacy left to him by his uncle, the Duke of Bridgewater, but his pride in his family name was unqualified.

Egerton's succession in 1823 to the Earldom and £40,000 a year allowed him to indulge his pride and his fancies. Everything that could be was embossed with the Bridgewater arms and crest – including the silver collars worn by his large assortment of dogs and cats. He styled himself a Prince of the Holy Roman Empire, a claim difficult to prove or disprove since the Empire, long a meaningless entity, had been formally dissolved in 1806.

Egerton was not much of a socialiser and often his only companions at dinner were two of his dogs – usually his favourites, Bijou and Biche. They, like all his other pets, were dressed in the height of Parisian fashion right down to their handmade boots. Linen napkins round their necks protected their clothes and a footman behind each chair made sure their wants were attended to. Of course the dogs were expected to display good manners, which is more than can be said for the Earl, who was something of a slob at table. Any of the 'guests' who failed to live up to the honour of dining with their master were condemned to the humiliation of wearing the yellow servants' livery and eating in the servants' hall for a week.

His carriage, emblazoned with the Bridgewater crest, pulled by four horses, and attended by liveried footmen, was often seen driving through Paris with half a dozen dogs reclining on silk cushions on their way to the Bois de Boulogne for a walk. If it rained a servant was on hand especially to shield them with an umbrella. Sometimes Egerton sent his carriage, fully attended, merely to convey a borrowed book back to a neighbour in proper Bridgewater style.

The Earl was a bit of a dandy. He suffered from a tremendous underbite and a very upturned chin, so his clothes had to be remarkable to distract attention from his unfortunate physiognomy. The same bootmaker who shod Egerton's pets had a standing order for a new pair of boots for the Earl himself. He wore each pair once only and employed a valet to keep the cast-offs arranged in the order in which they had been worn. That way a glance at any pair told him when, where and, as they were left uncleaned, in what weather he had worn them: Egerton's boots served him as a sort of diary.

Although he lived in France for over 30 years, Egerton never mastered French, which meant he had to converse with his scholarly friends in Latin. Even that was preferable to his later habit of ordering his secretary to entertain them by reading extracts from his long and ever changing will.

On the rare occasions when Egerton had friends to dine, they could reasonably expect a good meal since he employed, at no mean expense, the great chef, Viard. Egerton's favourite menu, however, was boiled beef and potatoes which he presented to his less-than-thrilled guests as a great English delicacy.

He missed English hunting and shooting even more than English boiled beef. With a few select friends, mounted on spirited horses, and dressed in pink coats, and with an imported fox, proper hounds, and a professional huntsman to sound the horn, Bridgewater gave miniature hunts in his Paris gardens. He also kept 300 each of rabbits, pigeons and partridges so that he could totter out into the grounds on the arm of a servant and bag his dinner.

His whims, which he always indulged, were often on a grand scale. Having once decided to remove for a season to the country, Egerton oversaw the ordeal of packing which went on for months. On the great day, the party set off in sixteen luggage-laden carriages led by one containing himself and his pets. Along with this came thirty servants on horseback. Only a few hours after this procession had left the Earl's house, neighbours saw it wearily returning. The change of plans had been occasioned by a substandard lunch which awakened the Earl to the hazards of travel.

In his will, Egerton left most of his estate to academic or charitable concerns and he directed that his house should be run for two months after his death as if he were still alive. Each servant received a mourning suit, a cocked hat and three pairs of worsted stockings. The dogs and cats were not mentioned.

Egerton is buried at Little Gaddesden Church in Hertfordshire. A monument designed to his instructions depicts a woman with a dolphin at her feet, a stork behind her and an elephant at her side.

Ellerton
Simeon

Simeon Ellerton was a man of considerable energy who thought
nothing of walking from his home in Durham to London on
errands for the local gentry. It was on such journeys that he gra-
dually formed the habit of collecting stones for a cottage he was
building; he generally carried one or two back on his head. By
the time he had completed his cottage he found that he could
walk more comfortably with a weight on his head than without.
For the rest of his life (at his death in 1799, he was 104) Ellerton
carried a heavy stone with him wherever he went. When asked
about it he explained, ''Tis to keep my hat on.'

Elwes
John

Elwes's father, Robert Meggott, a brewer in Southwark, died in
1718 when his son was less than four years old. His mother, Amy
Elwes Meggot, who had been left almost £100,000 is said to have
starved herself to death. At Westminster school, Elwes was a
good classical scholar but he was never to be seen afterwards
reading a book. He refused to educate his sons, on the principle
that 'putting things into people's heads is the sure way to take
money out of their pockets.' After school Elwes went to Geneva
to complete his education. Here he became one of the boldest
and best riders in Europe. He was also at this time introduced to
Voltaire, to whom he was reported to bear a remarkable
resemblance. Characteristically, Elwes was far more impressed
with the quality of the horses at his riding school than by the
genius of Voltaire.

Elwes did not yet display any of the miserly qualities which
characterised several members of his family. He indulged both
his voracious appetite and his fondness for gambling; one writer
noted, 'for many years Mr Elwes was known in all the fashionable circles of the metropolis.' This state of affairs began to
change when, after returning from Europe, Elwes was introduced to his maternal uncle, Sir Harvey Elwes, a very great
miser.

Although he was worth £250,000, Sir Harvey had an annual expenditure of less than £100. He ate little except partridges and fish that could be caught on his own property – paying for food was painful to him. Because he had few friends, he was not put to the expense of entertaining. His clothes came out of an ancient chest full of costumes belonging to his great-great grandfather.

As young Elwes entertained hopes of becoming the old man's heir, he endeavoured to please. For instance, on visits to Sir Harvey's Suffolk estate, Stoke College, he would stop first at a small inn nearby and change from his fashionable clothes to the rags his uncle favoured. He tamed his appetite by sneaking out to dine with a neighbour before sitting down with Sir Harvey to a miserable meal with one small glass of wine between them. John's behaviour so delighted Sir Harvey that he was made sole heir and on October 22 1763 inherited Elwes's name and his estate worth £250,000, including houses in Suffolk and Marcham, in Berkshire.

John Elwes combined the most miserly behaviour with high standards of honesty and compassion. He lost money in gambling, not only through his own bad fortune, but also because of his firmly held maxim that it is impossible to ask a gentleman for money, an attitude which led to him forfeiting large sums of money owed to him by less conscientious individuals.

He often gave aid, financial and otherwise, to friends and tenants, but spared himself no exertions to deliver it in the cheapest possible way. On one notable occasion Elwes, unsolicited, lent Lord Abingdon £7,000 to enable him to place a bet at Newmarket. On the day of the race, Elwes journeyed on horseback from Suffolk to the racetrack with nothing to eat for fourteen hours save a bit of pancake which he had put into his pocket two months earlier and which he swore to a startled companion was 'as good as new'.

Elwes's good nature is well illustrated by the story of his being hit during a shooting-party by a blast from the shotgun of an inexperienced marksman. 'I give you joy of your improvement!', Elwes exclaimed. 'I knew you would hit something by and by.'

Elwes's accomplishments include the building of Portman Place, Portman Square and a large part of Marylebone. During his twelve years as MP for Berkshire – although he refused to bear any of his election expenses and finally refused to stand again because of the money he lost in loans to fellow-members – Elwes was very conscientious about attending debates and voting independently. He had a reputation for unshakable integrity and was often called upon to settle disputes among his constituents, who placed great faith in his impartiality.

However, from the time when he first dressed in rags to humour his uncle, Elwes's behaviour became more and more remarkable. His idea of a journey was to mount one of his horses; take a hard-boiled egg in his pocket; choose a route with the fewest toll-gates, riding only on grass to save wear and tear on the horseshoes and refreshing himself and his mount by a stream to avoid the expense of an inn. On one occasion when he had ridden to and from London on an errand to help two old ladies in distress and they wanted to repay him for his expenses, a friend remarked 'give him sixpence and he gains twopence by the journey'.

Elwes's personal economies included going to bed when darkness fell so as to save on candles; rarely lighting a fire in his home, even when he was dripping wet from having walked home in the rain; and never allowing his shoes to be cleaned for fear of wearing them out. While in London, he stayed in any of his properties that happened to be empty. He kept only a few sticks of furniture which he moved from house to house as one was let and another became vacant. He once found a beggar's cast-off wig in a hedge, picked it up and wore it for two weeks. He always ate whatever he had in the cupboard, including maggot-ridden meat, before ordering new provisions.

Elwes's nephew, Col. Timms, found on one visit that the ceiling of his bedroom leaked. He was obliged to move the bed several times in order to find a dry corner. Mentioning this to his uncle the next morning, Timms received the calm reply, 'Aye, I don't mind it myself; but to those that do, that's a nice corner in the rain.'

One of Elwes's most characteristic combinations of miserliness and extravagance was his keeping a fine pack of fox hounds and a stable of hunters thought to be the best in England. This expensive interest was turned to good account by Elwes employing his huntsman to cook and serve at table as well as to look after the hounds and horses and milk the cows. He thus managed to keep the expense of his fox-hunting establishment to under £300 a year.

Elwes detested doctors and once, when he had cut both his legs badly walking home in the dark, he challenged the apothecary, 'I will take one leg and you shall take the other; you shall do what you please to yours, I will do nothing to mine.' To his great joy, Elwes won by a fortnight and the apothecary had to forfeit his fee.

In old age his memory worsened; his mind began to wander and he had fantasies about losing his money. One morning, after a sleepless night of worry, Elwes rushed to his bankers to apologise for having overdrawn his account by writing a cheque the previous day for £20. The apology was unnecessary as his balance at the time was £14,700.

Finally, Elwes went to live with one of his two natural sons, for whom he had a true fatherly feeling, and after his peaceful death on November 26 1789, the property worth £800,000 was divided between his sons and his nephew.

Eyre
Edward

Ned Eyre lived in Country Waterford with his 'daughters and heiresses', Miss Dapper and Miss Kitsey, two fine spotted labradors. He travelled in a glass coach drawn by four horses and dressed in brightly coloured silks and satins with contrasting linings. Satin shoes with jet buckles, a fan or a muff, and a complexion that owed a great deal to the paint box completed his toilette. Ned's cousin, Dorothea Herbert, remembered one occasion in the 1780s when he attended the races wearing a pink suit covered with diamante buttons and buckles.

Eyre never came downstairs before noon. He lived on tea, cold water, sweetmeats and pickles, but this meagre diet gave him enough energy to get through an immense fortune; although his property included a large part of Galway town, he was in debt most of his life.

Ned's whims were harmless, but often expensive. On the occasion of another visit to the races, he loaded his carriage with peaches and apricots for the Misses Dapper and Kitsey to enjoy on the journey. While staying in Galway he extended an invitation to 'all the beggars of Galway' to hot toast, tea and chocolate at his lodgings every morning. On the way home, Dorothea wrote, Ned 'stuffed our carriage with Galway fish which soon stank so abominably there was no bearing it.' Not all his pranks required a fat purse: having taken exception to the nurse in the next house for continually cooing over her family's new-born son, Eyre retaliated by dressing one of his servants up as an infant and dandling him on his knee in full view of the outraged nurse.

Ned's cousin, Col. Giles Eyre of the Galway Militia, was a wealthy and illiterate sportsman. He too ran through a great fortune, largely in the conventional manner – keeping a costly establishment including forty horses and seventy dogs – but he also had a costly whim to keep a plate of money outside his door so that beggars could help themselves. In 1811 Eyre stood for Parliament in Galway. His opponent, Mr Martin, known for his many duels as 'Hair Trigger Dick', was an astute politician. He offered to stand down from the race if Eyre would simply sign some meaningless document, but since Eyre could neither read nor write he was forced to decline Martin's offer and in spite of an expenditure of £80,000, Eyre lost the election.

Famous in Ireland for his daring exploits in the hunting field, Giles Eyre is commemorated in Charles Lever's ballad, *The Man for Galway*, the refrain of which is,

> *With debts galore, but fun far more*
> *Oh! That's the man for Galway.*

Lord Eyre of Eyrecourt, from whom Giles inherited his fortune, lived in a castle with windows that did not open, owned not one book, and presided at table every day from early afternoon to bedtime, working his way through great quantities of food and claret. The food, which never varied, was presented in a way that discouraged some guests: a slaughtered ox was hung up whole and diners were expected to help themselves.

Fitzgerald
John

 itzgeralds are all mad, but John is the maddest of the family, for he does not know it.' So wrote John's brother, Edward, the poet and translator, whose own behaviour was unremarkable except for his habit of using a very tall top hat as a receptacle for his tobacco, pipe and books, and tying it to his head with a handkerchief. Not so John. He was a wealthy man and a fervent evangelical preacher, whose sermons seldom failed to make an impact. Before beginning his talk, he would, with great ceremony, hand over his watch, handkerchief, keys and other personal belongings to various members of his audience. He often removed his boots and stockings as well, and if he became exceptionally carried away by his own rhetoric, he would take off further articles of clothing, never, however, exceeding the limits of decency. He generally delivered his sermons while standing on one foot, and might seize the lighted candles on the pulpit and gesticulate with them wildly to emphasise a point, spattering grease and hot wax all over the unfortunates sitting in the front row.

Fitzgerald was rarely asked to chair religious meetings as it soon became apparent that he generally forgot the existence of the main speaker in the course of an introduction that took up most of the evening. Even as a listener, his enthusiasm could be trying, for Fitzgerald's tendency to undress at moments of excitement applied to other people's speeches as well as his own.

Fitzgerald's wealth did not prevent him from taking the gospel seriously. He had several rooms in his house fitted out like a shop with shelves and drawers full of items to be given away and donated thousands of pounds, especially to alleviate the sufferings of miners. At the same time, there was in him a strong element of snobbery. He permitted only university graduates to sit with him at table or take him by the hand; to others he offered two fingers by way of a handshake. If he wanted to know the time, he rang for a servant to tell him, even though there was a clock in every room at Boulge Hall, the family estate in Suffolk which he inherited in 1854.

Fitzgerald's inability to make up his own mind made him a source of understandable exasperation to his brother, who once said that he regarded a letter from John stating the impossibility of a visit that day as an announcement of his imminent arrival. At the end of a visit to Edward, John often sent his carriage back empty, following it two minutes later in a hired coach.

His indecisiveness did have its beneficial side, however. There is a story of John Fitzgerald waiting for a train at a station in Wales. The stationmaster spotted the train and announced, 'The train's coming, sir'. There was no reply. Presently he announced, 'The train's in, sir.' Fitzgerald remained immobile. After a few more minutes the stationmaster remarked, 'The train's gone, sir'. Fitzgerald's only comment was to his servant: 'Take up those things,' he said, pointing to the baggage. He led the way back to the hotel, where later in the evening news came that the passengers on the train had been involved in a fatal accident.

Fordyce
George

Dr Fordyce, who became a highly esteemed physician and lecturer, got off to a slow start with his career. His shabby appearance and curt bedside manner didn't win him many patients, although his unorthodox treatment had some surprising results.

On one occasion called to the sick bed of a titled lady, when he had had too much to drink, he found it impossible to take her pulse as his own was so unsteady. In frustration he cursed himself, muttering, 'Drunk, by Jove!' and left her with some harmless medicaments. The next day he was again summoned to see her and went, fearing her wrath at his unprofessional behaviour. Instead she begged his forgiveness, confessed that his diagnosis had been correct, gave him £100, and vowed to mend her ways.

Fordyce was of the opinion that eating and sleeping occupied too much of our time. He could do with very little sleep and a study of the eating habits of the lion convinced him that one meal a day was sufficient for men as well as for the King of Beasts. Accordingly, for twenty years he followed an unaltered pattern. At four o'clock every afternoon he entered Dolly's

Chop House in Paternoster Row where, while waiting for his one and a half pounds of rump steak he attended to an appetizer of half a chicken or a plate of boned fish. With his meal he drank a tankard of strong ale, a quarter-pint of brandy, and a bottle of port. Economy was not his aim in this regimen, for Dolly's prices were not cheap. As Caulfield notes, in *Portraits of Remarkable Persons*, 'many an alderman and wealthy citizen were satisfied to pay double for their chops, or basin of soup to be waited on and gratified with the sight of Dolly's fascinating female attendants.'

After leaving Dolly's, Dr Fordyce went to three coffee-houses, one after another, taking a brandy and water at each, and then returned home. He died of gout in 1802 at the age of sixty-six.

'*Mad Jack*'
Fuller
John

'Mad Jack', or 'Honest Jack', as he liked to be called, was MP
from 1801 to 1812 for Rose Hill (now Brightling) in Sussex. His
political nature was fiery, to say the least. He more than once
caused an uproar in the House and had to be ejected forcibly
when he referred to the Speaker as 'the insignificant little fellow
in the wig'. He was a large man (twenty-two stone and nicknamed 'Hippo') with a bluff manner, a sense of humour and no
pretensions. Declining Pitt's offer of a peerage, he said, 'I was
born Jack Fuller and Jack Fuller I'll die.' He loved Rose Hill and
commissioned Turner to paint five pictures of the area. When
unemployment was high Fuller built walls on his property just as
a means of providing jobs for the local people.

His memory endures, however, chiefly through his love of
follies. He erected a domed rotunda and a 'hermit's tower' on his
estate, not to mention the Brightling Needle, a sixty-five foot
high obelisk which to this day remains a Sussex landmark. The
Sugar Loaf Folly at Dallington was built as the result of a bet
Fuller made with a neighbour that he could see the distinctive
conical spire of Dallington Church from his window at Rose
Hill. When he found on returning home that he could do no such
thing, Fuller, in a joking attempt to maintain his credit, built a
forty-foot replica of the spire on a nearby hill to give the illusion
of a half visible church.

His masterpiece is undoubtedly the pyramidal mausoleum he
had built for himself in Brightling Churchyard from the designs
of Sir Robert Smirke, the architect of the British Museum. The
reason Fuller gave for declining to be buried conventionally was
his fear of being eaten by his relatives. 'The worms', he
explained, 'would eat me, the ducks would eat the worms and
my relative would eat the ducks.' Inside, it is said, Fuller sits in
an armchair wearing a top hat and holding a bottle of claret.
Around him broken glass is scattered so that 'when the devil
comes to claim his own he might at least cut his feet'.

Gainsborough
Jack

ainsborough, although he was also an artist in his own way, never achieved the fame or fortune of his brother, Thomas. He was an inventor, whose work was distinguished by its imagination and lack of practical purpose. His inventions included a cuckoo that sang all year long, a haystack that walked, and a pair of copper wings that earned him the nickname 'the Sudbury Daedalus'. But it was while he was still a boy that he came up with what must have been the most original of his achievements. A neighbour, Colonel Addison, remembered being called round to look at a remarkable species of apple tree. Jack had covered every single one of the apples with dough 'which by means of a chafing dish of hot coals and a saucepan he had contrived to parboil', so that the astonished Colonel found himself looking at a tree weighed down with dozens of apple dumplings.

Galton
Sir Francis

Francis Galton was a man of science and a pioneer in many fields. He established conclusively that fingerprints are a reliable test of identity; he developed a way of graphically recording weather patterns; he invented the cyclometer to record speed and mileage for bicyclists; and, under the influence of the ideas of his cousin, Charles Darwin, he developed the science of eugenics or selective breeding.

His intellectual curiosity led him, while studying medicine at King's College, London, to go through the *Pharmacopoeia* in alphabetical order, trying out the drugs on himself to discover their various effects. His experiments with aniseed and belladonna went off quite smoothly but the purgative effects of castor oil led him to abandon this road to learning.

Galton deplored guesswork in science and was determined to quantify anything he could. In his Beauty Map of the British

Isles, he charted the incidence of beauty – as measured by a system best known to himself – throughout Great Britain and found that the prettiest women were in London and the ugliest in Aberdeen. The map was a bestseller in Aberdeen. He also developed a system for numerically measuring the degree of resemblance between two people.

Galton began his career by travelling widely in Africa and his guide to mounting expeditions, *The Art of Travel*, contains many invaluable tips. 'A raw egg,' he tells us, 'broken into a boot before putting it on, greatly softens the leather.' To track a bee to its hive, Galton suggests merely catch it and tie a feather to its leg so that its flight will be easy to follow. Galton recommends a pair of opera glasses and an ear trumpet as essential equipment in the bush. He describes how in 1850 he managed not to lose face in a meeting with an elaborately dressed and decorated Zambesi chieftain by coming forward in full hunting pink, mounted on an ox.

One device Galton didn't mention in his book was his Universal Patent Ventilating Hat, which, in later years, he was seldom without. This was a top hat with a moveable crown. A valve was attached by a tube to a rubber bulb which, when squeezed, caused the valve to lift the crown, thus allowing the overheated head to breathe. Galton acknowledged that his hat looked out of place at smart dinner parties, but said it was preferable to 'falling in a fit upon the floor'.

Graham
James

In 1779, James Graham, the most inventive quack in British history, opened his 'Temple of Health' at the Adelphi, London. Here, to large and fashionable audiences, he gave demonstrations of his 'Celestial Bed' – a night spent on which guaranteed fertility to childless couples. His assistant on these occasions was a young woman described as 'the rosy, athletic, and truly gigantic Goddess of Health and of Hymen', a role that was played for a short time by Emma Lyons, later Lady Hamilton.

Graham's rooms were full of ingeniously constructed and elaborately decorated apparatus. His 'electrical throne', is a good example of his taste in furnishings: it consisted of a circular platform, covered by a fringed piece of crimson silk damask, and supported by massive glass pillars which stood on burnished gold bases. This was connected by brass rods and a fluted gold column to an electric conductor – which was itself surrounded by four Ionic columns festooned with garlands of artificial flowers – and mounted on three enamelled and gilt glass columns.

Sitting behind green silk curtains, Graham received patients, prescribed his 'Imperial pills', advised on how to live for 150 years, and offered samples of his Elixir of Life for £1,000.

Eventually, Graham ran into debt and had to leave London. He spent some time in Edinburgh and touring the provinces and by 1787 had acquired a wholly new character: he signed himself 'the Servant of the Lord, OWL' (Oh Wonderful Love) and had adopted a system of dating based on 'the first year of the New Jerusalem Church'. He became a vegetarian; gave up alcohol; and slept on a hair mattress.

In 1790, four years before his death, Graham, who, although still a prophet of the New Jerusalem Church, was not yet in a position to give up his commercial interests, invented earth-bathing. He acquired a new Goddess of Health and with her gave demonstrations of the art. Watchers paid one guinea to see the two of them, packed in warm earth for up to eight hours at a time, naked, but with their hair curled and powdered, appearing 'not unlike two fine, full-grown cauliflowers'. The poet, George Dyer, desperate to read his work aloud, found them a convenient captive audience.

Not everyone laughed at Graham's nostrums: one grateful patient, cured perhaps by a series of earthbaths, gave Graham an annuity which made his last days comfortable.

Halstead
John

alstead, a retired salesman from Yorkshire, began in 1936 decorating the outside of his cottage at Burnedge, Broad Lane in Rochdale. By the time he had finished, the walls were completely covered with oyster shells, old iron bedsteads, broken tiles, cows' horns, framed photographs, cups, plates, and saucers, and whole tea pots with flowers growing out of them. Neighbourhood children collected fragments of pottery for Mr Halstead and were rewarded with a spot of cement and a bit of wall to cover. The Shell House became a local wonder and an attraction for weekend sightseers, though Halstead never made nor sought to make any money in this way. To celebrate the Coronation of George VI, Halstead outlined all the windows and the roof with strings of electric lights painted red, white and blue.

Mrs Edna Buckley, who lived nearby as a child, remembered Mr Halstead as a great orator. 'He worshipped the sun god and above the front door was the word *Temporiparendum* worked in scraps of blue and white pottery. This, he said, meant 'we move with the times'. . . . We would often hear Mr Halstead chopping up his pottery in the early hours of the morning as he used to rise with the sun.'

After his death in 1940, the Shell House was sold for £25; the new owners destroyed Mr Halstead's legacy in order to modernise the house.

Hamilton
Charles

Charles Hamilton's estate at Pains Hill, Surrey, was one of the first and most impressive examples of picturesque landscaping, a style much in vogue in the mid-eighteenth century, inspired by the paintings of Claude Lorraine and Poussin and highlighted by strategically placed gothic ruins. Pains Hill had more than its share of these scattered throughout the grounds along with numerous cliffs, waterfalls, tunnels, and Italian and Alpine vistas.

There was a deserted abbey, with hexagonal turrets, carefully constructed to look weatherbeaten; a Greek temple designed by Batty Langley, midwife to so many gothic wonders; and a two-storey grotto built on a dead tree and intended to serve as a hermitage. As a finishing touch to this romantic picture, Charles Hamilton wanted a real hermit to live in his grotto and wander through the grounds, providing spiritual inspiration for his family and friends.

Mr Hamilton placed an advertisement saying that he would pay £700 to any man who would stay seven years in the hermitage and observe certain conditions. These were that he must not talk to anyone and must never shave or cut his hair or his nails. The successful applicant was to be provided with a Bible, a long robe, spectacles, a prayer mat, an hourglass, and food and water. A prospective hermit eventually came forth, but after three weeks he succumbed to loneliness and a fondness for beer. No successor was appointed.

Marquess of Abercorn
Hamilton
John James

John James Hamilton, 9th Earl and 1st Marquess of Abercorn, was a man well aware of the esteem due to his position and not inclined to tolerate those who forgot it. Indeed, such forgetfulness must have been rare since Abercorn went to some lengths to make his exalted station clear to all. Travelling in Italy as plain Mr Hamilton before he inherited the title from his uncle, he had cards printed which read 'D'Hamilton, Comte Hereditaire d'Abercorn'. When someone remarked upon the similarity of his livery to that of the Royal Family, he replied 'My family took it from *them*? No, it was the livery of the Hamiltons before the House of Brunswick had a servant to put it on.'

After his first wife died, Abercorn wanted to marry his cousin, Miss Cecil Hamilton. First, however, he persuaded Pitt, then Prime Minister, to raise her to the status of an Earl's daughter (although she had four older sisters who were not so elevated) so that he might not marry beneath himself. The union, noble though both parties were, was not a success, but when Lord Abercorn discovered that his lady was on the verge of eloping, he begged her to take the family carriage to meet her lover 'as it ought never to be said that Lady Abercorn left her husband's roof in a hack chaise'. Later, Abercorn married Lady Ann Hatton, described rather melodramatically by Lady Holland as 'a frolicsome Irish widow, very pretty, very foolish and very debauched', and acquired the facetious nickname, 'Bluebeard'.

Sir Walter Scott, an old family friend of the Hamiltons, used often to tell the following story about them as an example of a style of living which was rare even at that time. On his way to visit Abercorn in Carlisle, Scott came upon a procession of five carriages, numerous outriders, and a man on horseback wearing the blue ribbon of the Knights of the Garter. This was Abercorn and his family out for a drive. The small village of Longtown had been galvanised to receive this illustrious party for dinner. Since a common public house could not be relied upon to provide food of the quality demanded by Abercorn, his majordomo and cook had been sent on ahead to oversee preparations. Goose from the village lake made the main course; crockery was commandeered from the inn; and the rest of the village provided linen, fruits, vegetables and preserves.

Presumably the travellers brought with them their own supply of rose-water, for Lord Abercorn would not accept anything from a servant who had not just dipped his fingers in a bowl of rose-water. The housemaids had to wear white kid gloves while making his bed.

Lord Abercorn insisted that everyone with a claim to fame or beauty be invited to stay at his house, Bentley Priory, in Stanmore. Once there, guests were free to do exactly as they chose: the Marquess's stables, his park and his servants were at their command. Only one restriction was imposed: they were not to speak to their host. If a guest happened to pass Abercorn during the day, he was to ignore him. Only at table would he indulge in conversation with his guests. Sometimes even this brief communication was impossible. When *Thaddeus of Warsaw*, a novel by Jane Porter-Hyde, was published, Lord Abercorn was keen to get her to the Priory. Lady Blessington records him as saying, 'Gad, we must have these Porters. Write, my dear Lady A!' When the Porters replied that they could not afford the journey, Abercorn sent a cheque. The long-awaited guests duly arrived, but Abercorn, having watched their entrance from behind a curtain, decided he did not like the look of them and left the house until their visit had ended.

Hamilton
Robert

Hamilton, an absent-minded professor of mathematics at Aberdeen University, was checked by a member of his household staff every morning before he set off to teach to ensure that he was fully dressed. But, in spite of periodic lapses, Hamilton was – in his own way – perfectly capable of looking after himself. Although mathematics was his first love, Hamilton was appointed in 1799 to the chair of natural philosophy at Aberdeen. A Mr Copland, a man with a philosophical bent, was at the time Aberdeen's professor of mathematics. Somehow Hamilton and Copland, in an entirely private deal, agreed to switch chairs, classes and students. The unofficial arrangement lasted for eighteen years until Hamilton was formally appointed to the chair of mathematics.

Hamilton's students were fond of him, but tempted to take advantage of his distracted manner. They used to throw peas at the professor as he wrote his equations on the board. This did not in the least disturb him; he merely sheltered the back of his head with his hand and went on writing. One day, however, a prankster went too far and threw a toy cracker which, exploding near Hamilton's head, frightened him. He bolted out of the room, thinking that he had narrowly missed being hit by gunshot. As he stood in the corridor trembling, a delegation of his students came out to apologise and beg him to return. 'Gentlemen,' he said, 'I have no objection to the peas, for I can easily protect myself with my hand, but I entreat you to spare my life.' The students explained the mistake, promising to restrict themselves to peas in future, and Hamilton went back to his board.

Hanger
George

Having fought three duels, married a gypsy, and been wounded in the American War of Independence, George Hanger retired from the army at the age of twenty-two and devoted himself to drinking, racing, gambling and whoring. Not surprisingly, he soon became a boon companion of the Prince of Wales. Like the Prince, Hanger was a man of fashion, the first person in England to wear a satin coat. Apart from his retirement half-pay, which barely covered his tailor's bill, Hanger had two sources of income: gambling and moneylenders. He would bet on anything and once laid a wager on the outcome of a ten-mile race between twenty geese and twenty turkeys, losing £500 when the turkeys dropped out after 3 miles.

In 1798, after fifteen years of living beyond his means, Hanger was made a prisoner of the King's Bench. He stayed there for eighteen months and, unlike those debtors whose wealthy friends contrived to maintain them in style within their private cells, Hanger experienced the true degradation and squalor of life in a debtor's prison. He later wrote an eloquent condemnation of the soul-destroying conditions in such prisons. When some friends eventually procured his release by paying off his debts, this pillar of the beau monde immediately embarked on a new career. He became a coal merchant. Society was aghast, and a number of friends offered to set him up in a more acceptable line of business. But Hanger, far from finding his new position a humiliation, positively revelled in embarrassing his fashionable friends by drawing attention to his changed circumstances.

Hanger sold coal for fourteen years. Then on the death in 1814 of his brother, George acceded to the estates and title of Baron Coleraine. He despised inherited titles and corrected anyone who used his, saying, 'Plain George Hanger if you please.' This attitude and other unorthodox opinions finally put an end to friendly relations with his old companion, now George IV.

Hanger was quite genuine about his democratic ideas. As his fourteen years as a coal seller demonstrated, he had no desire to hold himself aloof from the lower orders. Shortly after he succeeded to the title, the artist J T Smith witnessed this scene between him and an old woman who sold apples in the Portland Road. Hanger saw her packing up her things in preparation for her tea break. 'Don't balk trade', he said, 'Leave your things on the table as they are: I will mind your shop till you come back.' Intrigued, Smith loitered and watched Hanger selling apples to passers-by. On the woman's return, Hanger turned over his takings. 'Well, mother, I have taken threepence half-penny for you. Did your daughter Nancy drink tea with you?'

By this time Hanger was quite well known, not so much for his past exploits as for the controversial views set forth in his highly readable autobiography, *The Life, Adventures, and Opinions of Col. George Hanger*. In it Hanger offers a good deal of advice to women. He insists that they should settle affairs of honour by duelling amongst themselves, instead of involving men. He recommends, when eloping, leaving through a window, rather than a door. 'It will impress your lover with a respect for your heroism, and ever establish you, in his opinion, as a woman of true spirit, courage, and spunk.' He applauds the fashion for loose gowns, which he says are 'admirably suited either for a young lady to conceal a big belly, or for a shop-lifter to hide a bale of goods.'

He advised clergymen to supplement their income by hiring out the blind men in their parishes to beggar-women who find that a genuinely handicapped companion exerts a greater pull on the heart-strings and purse-strings of the contributing public than even a child or a dog. And he advocated a tax on Scotsmen who spent more than six months of the year south of the border.

Hardy
Godfrey Harold

Although he was a mathematician of genius who, through his own work and that of his pupils, had a considerable influence on twentieth-century mathematics, Hardy was somewhat less at home with twentieth-century technology. He refused to use a watch, found quills more congenial than fountain pens, and if he had to use the telephone at all, would simply shout his message into the mouthpiece and hang up, denying that he could hear anything through the receiver.

In spite of his later achievements in mathematics, Hardy always felt that his education had been inadequate 'I could have been a first-class batsman if only I had had the proper coaching at Winchester,' he would complain. He settled instead for a fellowship at Trinity College, Cambridge, where he spent much of his time watching cricket. He always appeared on the grounds with three or four thick sweaters, an umbrella and a large pile of books. This outfit, which he called his 'anti-God battery', was designed to deceive God into thinking that he expected rain and looked forward to getting on with some work and, according to Hardy, it was excellent insurance against bad weather.

Hardy was, in fact, a determined atheist, and for many years scored for the Devil while the Rev. F. A. Simpson, himself a much loved college character, scored for God, in a competition in which points were awarded to the supernatural agent who seemed most responsible for the day's news. Remarkably, the score was more or less equal, possibly because Simpson took the precaution of subscribing to a number of clerical papers.

Simpson is remembered for his brilliant and carefully prepared sermons. One Sunday preaching at King's he noticed in the congregation a number of undergraduates who had heard him give the same sermon the previous week at Trinity. Looking down at them he said, 'And may I remind certain people that it is better to hear a good sermon twice than to hear a bad one once.'

As an old man, Simpson was asked to speak at Mervyn Stockwood's installation as the Bishop of London. The night before the ceremony Simpson was entertained to dinner by the Archbishop of Canterbury, the Rev. Fisher, and his wife. Simpson was in a state of nerves over his part in the next day's ceremony, but the evening went smoothly, with the highly strung don on his best behaviour. As Simpson took his leave of Dr and Mrs Fisher, he added quietly, 'And may I just say, had you offered me alcohol, I should have refused it.'

Hardy had a brilliant collaborator in Ramanujau, the self-taught Indian mathematician whom he had helped to bring to England in 1914. Ramanujau, who had been working as a clerk in Madras when he began a correspondence with Hardy, became fatally ill with tuberculosis soon after being made a Fellow of the Royal Society in 1918. Hardy often visited him in hospital. One day, depressed by his friend's condition and at a loss for conversation, he nervously stammered out, 'The number of my taxi was 1729. It seemed to me rather a dull number.' Ramanujau, much distressed by his off-hand remark replied, 'No Hardy! No Hardy! It is a very interesting number. It is the smallest number expressible as the sum of two cubes in two different ways.'

Hawker
Robert

It was primarily a poet's need for solitude that drove Robert Hawker to take holy orders and move to the quiet Cornish parish of Morwenstow, where for the next forty years he lived very much as he pleased.

Feeling that clerical black made him look like 'a waiter out of place or an unemployed undertaker', he devised a working costume of a brown cassock with velvet cuffs, a floppy tie and a black velvet hat. Later on, becoming more adventurous, he could often be seen wearing a three-quarter length purple coat, blue jersey, scarlet gauntlets and yellow poncho.

Hawker and his wife always tried to wear matching or complementary outfits. After thirty-one years of a very happy marriage Mrs Hawker, who was her husband's godmother and twenty-two years his senior, died. Hawker, though much distressed, carried on their interest in fashion by wearing a pink fez to her funeral.

In 1849 he began restoring the church and vicarage. He rebuilt five of the chimneys at the rectory as replicas of the towers of his favourite churches, but remained undecided about the sixth until, in his own words, 'I bethought me of my mother's tomb; and there it is, in its exact shape and dimensions.'

He removed the panelling from the pulpit on the grounds that, 'the people ought to see the priest's feet' and he refused to alter the very awkward, narrow passageway which gave onto the pulpit because he enjoyed teasing visting priests who got stuck in it. The church roof was retiled, not properly with slate, but with wood. Hawker knew that this wouldn't last as long, but he insisted that bad materials as well as good ones should be used as a symbol of the Church's welcome to sinners as well as saints.

Inside, the church didn't always present an edifying picture – the altar covered with spent matches, and cat and dog hairs everywhere. Hawker let his own and other people's pets into church, sometimes even into the pulpit while he was preaching. Once when a parishioner was shooing a dog out during a service, he reprimanded her, 'Let him be, Mrs Mills, there were dogs in the Ark.' There is a story that he excommunicated one of his cats for catching a mouse on Sunday, but Hawker had a reputation as a friend to animals. When one of his old cassocks was used to dress a scarecrow, the result was disastrous. Recognising the uniform of their protector, the birds flocked to the scarecrow in anticipation of a hand-out and did substantial damage to the nearby crops.

On his deathbed – as might have been predicted by those who observed his fondness for elaborate and richly embroidered vestments in the Roman style – Robert Hawker, forty-four years an Anglican priest, converted to Catholicism.

Hirst
Jemmy

Even as a young boy, woefully out of place in a boarding-school for future clergymen, Jemmy Hirst was noted for his interest in animals. He got into trouble for harnessing his teacher's pig and training it to jump hurdles. His expulsion, however, was due to another prank. Jemmy threw a fishing line out of an upper window with such unerring accuracy that he managed to hook the schoolmaster's wig as that gentleman passed below.

Giving up the idea of schooling him, Jemmy's father, a farmer in Rawcliffe, Yorkshire, sent him away as apprentice to a tanner. In 1756, after a brief engagement that ended when his betrothed, his master's daughter, died, Jemmy returned to Rawcliffe and made his fortune as a speculator in farm produce.

He had maintained his legendary love of animals: his best friends were an otter and a tame fox, and he had a pet bear called Nicholas. Hirst turned out regularly with Lord Beaumont's foxhounds on his favourite mount, a bull named Jupiter. He tried to train a litter of pigs as foxhounds, but the experiment was only a qualified success due largely to the incessant grunting.

Hirst was also something of an inventor. His carriage was fitted with a device that measured mileage according to the number of wheel rotations. He designed a windmill for cutting up turnips, and, less successfully, a pair of feathered wings that earned him a dunking in the Humber when he strapped them on and took off from the mast of a boat. Later he attached sails to his carriage and travelled from Rawcliffe to Pontefract before crashing into a draper's shop.

A familiar face at the Doncaster races, Jemmy gathered crowds as he stepped down from his multi-coloured wicker-work carriage which was drawn by four Andalusian mules and fitted with a wine cellar and a double bed. Wearing a lambskin cap nine feet in circumference, and otter-skin coat, a waistcoat of drake's feathers, patchwork breeches, red and white striped stockings and yellow boots, he handed out his own private currency – coloured banknotes of his own design worth five halfpence each.

It was in the same outfit that Hirst appeared at Court in response to an invitation from George III. His initial reaction was

to delay the visit because, as he airily explained to Lord Beaumont, 'I am very busy just now training an otter to fish', but his curiosity and his vanity got the better of him and he went to London within the week.

Prior to being presented to the King, Jemmy was subjected by Beaumont to a crash course in court etiquette. He had no patience for such things and finally exclaimed in exasperated tones, 'Damn your fuss and ceremonies. . . I didn't seek his acquaintance – he must take me as I am.'

Hirst's visit aroused a great deal of curiosity. The crowds that followed him to Court were amazed by his wicker carriage and strange clothes, as were the nobles waiting to meet him. The Duke of Devonshire collapsed with laughter, but Jemmy chose to believe that the cause of the collapse was an attack of hysterics and he insisted upon helpfully loosening his neckcloth, slapping his cheeks, and throwing a glass of water in his face.

Brought face to face with George III, Hirst, who refused to bow to anybody, manfully held out his hand. The King, highly entertained, shook hands with him, spent some time asking about his inventions and his animals, and sent him away with his carriage filled with wine from the Royal cellars.

At home Jemmy frequently gave parties for the young and old people in his village. Three blasts on a horn summoned the youngsters for a dance at which Hirst would play the fiddle; six blasts signalled a party for older people. On these occasions he loved to show his guests his collection of coffins. One served as a liquor cabinet; another, which visitors were invited to try for size, had folding doors, glass windows, and a bell to summon servants. As they stepped inside, the doors automatically closed and locked. Men had to surrender a penny, women a garter, before they were allowed out.

In his will Hirst left instructions that his coffin be borne to the grave by twelve old maids to the accompaniment of a fiddler and a bagpiper. Since only two women could be found to swear to their maidenly status, widows were employed instead. The vicar ruled out the fiddler and made the bagpiper play solemn music, but there was nothing he could do about the army of colourful sporting characters who followed Jemmy to the graveyard.

James
Venetia

 udging by her background – she was born a Cavendish-Bentinck and had married an American millionaire – Venetia James might have been expected to be extravagant. But although she entertained a good deal, she did so according to principles of domestic economy so strict that they often inhibited her social ambitions. At one of her own house parties, at Coton in Northamptonshire, she exclaimed, 'Only one baronet and one viscount! What a mangy weekend!'

Not as mangy as the greasy parcel of bacon left over from the weekend that, according to her great-nephew Christopher Simon Sykes, she often returned to her butcher on a Monday morning. Venetia always preferred to deal on a sale or return basis. It was a rare meal at the James house that did not produce quite substantial leftovers – due largely to her highly developed methods of limiting the size of the portions served. One night, after a miracle of carving by means of which ten people dined from a single chicken, Mrs James passed a note to her butler which read DCSC (Don't Cut Second Chicken).

On Fridays Catholics could expect a warm welcome at Coton because their religion required them to eat fish, which was cheaper than meat. If meat was offered at all, it was strictly rationed, with Mrs James hissing as the diners were served, 'Fish for the Papists! Fish for the Papists!'

The James economy drive demanded sacrifices from family, household staff, and pets, as well as friends. Audrey Coates, her niece, was surprised to be invited in to tea, while passing Venetia's house in London. As she ventured in, she heard her aunt call out to the housekeeper, 'Emily, if the cat has left any of its milk, bring it up for Mrs Coates.' A veterinarian, summoned to attend to one of the family dogs, was asked to take a look at an ailing maid when he was finished, since ordinary doctors were 'a ridiculous waste of money'. On another occasion, strolling through Hyde Park with Sir Charles Degraz, Venetia asked him to pick up a dead sparrow lying in the grass. He carried it back to the house where she called out, 'Emily, discommand the cat's meat. Sir Charles has bought her a fallen bird.'

Violet Trefusis told a story about travelling back to Coton with Venetia after she had bought a new hat in London. Having bypassed several trains in order to wait for one with third-class compartments – the only way Venetia James would travel – they found themselves on a station platform waiting to make a connection for Rugby. It was raining, and Venetia lifted up her skirts to protect her new purchase, thus revealing to the world her red flannel petticoats and bloomers. The stationmaster protested that she was indecent, but Venetia was unmoved. 'My good man,' she drawled from under her skirts, 'what you see is old, but the hat is new.'

Jennings
Henry Constantine

Jennings was an avid collector, deeply attached to his 'finds'. For six months after he had acquired a beautiful statue of Venus, he insisted that it be placed at the head of his dinner table and attended by two liveried footmen.

Painting, sculpture, books, prints, stuffed birds, shells, precious stones, and coins were but a few of his obsessions. Not surprisingly, his expenditure frequently exceeded his income, with the result that he often found himself bankrupt, and forced to sell off collections in order to be released from jail. Finally he discovered a way of breaking this vicious cycle: in 1816, when he was next imprisoned, Jennings decided not to part with his collection, but to settle down in jail, surrounded by his treasures for the rest of his life.

For Jennings, one drawback of ending his days behind bars was the prospect of receiving a conventional burial. He detested the thought of physical decay and was believed by his neighbours to keep an oven in his house for his own cremation so that he could be spared the indignity of slow disintegration. His regimen for keeping in good physical condition was strenuous. Three hundred times every morning and evening he flourished a heavy broad sword tipped with lead at both ends. He then mounted an artificial horse, 'composed of leather and inflated with wind like a pair of bellows', on which he took exactly 1000 gallops. One result of this was an extreme bow-leggedness which, one observer remarked, made him appear to be walking sideways.

Jones
Morgan

During his forty-three years as vicar of Blewbury, near Didcot, Jones developed a reputation for inventive miserliness rivalling that of an earlier local celebrity, John Elwes (*q.v.*). Like Elwes, Jones had a healthy appetite when dining at someone else's expense. He got his bacon from a local farmer, extending the transaction over three visits – to order, fetch and pay for it – with each visit perfectly timed to enable Jones to take tea *and* supper with the farmer and his family.

He wore the same coat and hat for the whole period of his tenure in Blewbury, from 1781 to 1824. Somehow the coat has survived and is kept today in a glass case by one of the parishioners. In this much mended garment one can clearly see Jones's ingenuity with a needle and thread; he turned it first inside out and then practically upside down by using pieces of the lining and tail to patch the jacket.

His hat fell to pieces, after twenty-five years, but Jones salvaged it by attaching the brim of a hat he found on a scarecrow to the still-intact crown of his own hat. This mongrel – the crown was black and the brim brown – carried him through to his retirement. One way in which Jones reduced wear and tear on his clothes was by the simple expedient of never washing them.

In spite of his peculiarities, Jones was liked by his parishioners, for his good nature and peaceable disposition. His sermons, written on old pieces of sandpaper or used marriage licences, were well prepared, and, in the pulpit, wearing a surplice, he looked quite respectable. A visitor to the village walking home from church with a friend asked him why he had tipped his hat to 'that old beggar man' and was astonished to hear that he was the vicar to whom they had just been reverently listening.

When Jones retired he would have liked, after forty-three years, to have stayed on in Blewbury, but as there was no one who could keep him for free and he could not bear to think of parting with any of his money, he was forced to fall back on relatives he barely knew in Wales, promising to remember them in his will. He died at age eighty, soon after retiring, leaving his heirs a fortune of £18,000.

Kirwan
Richard

irwan lived a quiet life as a chemist and scholar. He enjoyed an independent income of 014,000 a year and after his wife died in 1765, he was able to arrange his life just as it suited him. He dined alone and ate only ham and milk. Apart from mealtimes, Kirwan enjoyed company and was known as a brilliant conversationalist. At his twice weekly soirées, he received his guests while reclining on a couch before a fire, wearing a hat and two coats. At seven o'clock the door knocker was removed so that new arrivals would not disrupt the flow of conversation, and at nine precisely the guests were expected to leave. As soon as their time was up Kirwan removed his shoes and knee buckles as a pointed reminder to any lingerers that the party was over.

When he had to go out, Kirwan, whose health was delicate, took precautions. First he stood in front of a roaring fire with his coat open for a few minutes in order to catch the heat. Once outside, he walked at a good clip and refused to speak for fear of releasing some of his stored heat. And no matter where he went – to a scientific meeting or a court function – he always kept his hat on indoors. Asked why he never entered a church, Kirwan said he could not think of removing his hat.

His life revolved around the books and papers which spilled off tables and bookshelves and lay in piles on the floor, on chairs, everywhere in his home. His chief companion was a faithful manservant, named Pope, who now shares Kirwan's grave. Although he loved animals, and kept six pet dogs and an eagle trained to sit on his shoulder, Kirwan hated flies so much that he gave his servants a bonus for each dead fly they produced.

He rose at 4.00 a.m. every day during the summer; in the winter he allowed himself to sleep in until half past four. Kirwan cannot have enjoyed very sound sleep, although his nights were probably more restful than poor Pope's, whose duty it was to rise several times during the night and pour tea down the sleeping Kirwan's throat, all too often drenching his hair, eyes, nose and bedclothes in the process.

Sadly, after all his precautions over his health, Kirwan tried the fashionable remedy of starving a cold – with fatal results.

Complications set in and he died soon after at the age of seventy-nine.

Kitchiner
William

Dear Sir,

The honour of your company is requested to dine with the Committee of Taste, on Wednesday next, the 10th instant.

The specimens will be placed upon the table at five o'clock precisely, when the business of the day will immediately commence. I have the honour to be your most obedient servant.
William Kitchiner, Secretary
Eta Beta Pi

Members and guests of the dining club Eta Beta Pi had to observe the strict guidelines laid down by its founder and secretary, Kitchiner. Invitations not answered within twenty-four hours of issuance were withdrawn. Dinner was served on the stroke of five and latecomers were never admitted, 'the Secretary having represented that the perfections of several of the preparations is so exquisitely evanescent that the delay of one minute after their arrival at the meridian of concoction will render them no longer worthy of men of taste.' Latecomers were lucky only to be deprived of their meal; Kitchiner felt that they should have to contribute to a Fund for the Benefit of Decaying Cooks.

Though he was known chiefly as an epicure, Kitchiner had a wide range of interests. Besides his cookery books, he wrote pamphlets such as 'The Pleasure of Making a Will' and 'The Pleasure of Early Rising'. His essay on locomotion recommended travelling on cow back for the convenience of having a constant supply of fresh milk.

One of his contemporaries said that Kitchiner's chief enjoyment was 'to invent odd things and give them odd names'. One of these inventions was the 'portable magazine of taste'. This was an essential piece of equipment for epicures and invalids who did not wish their specialised palates to be a burden to friends with whom they were invited to dine. Besides the twenty-eight bottles of such basic condiments as Dr Kitchiner's own Wow-Wow sauce (a mixture of port, pickled cucumbers, capers and mustard), essence of celery, curacao, lemon peel and pickled walnuts, the magazine was fitted out with the bare minimum of equipment needed to rescue a badly prepared meal: a set of weights and measures, scales, pestle and mortar and nutmeg grater.

Kolkhurst
George Alfred

Although for thirty-seven years Kolkhurst was a Reader in Spanish at Oxford University, he always felt that his real vocation was for the life of a nineteenth-century aesthete. He was a three-year-old child living with his parents in Chile when that century drew to a close, and cannot be said to have had much personal knowledge of the aesthetic movement; nevertheless, he did his best to conform to Wildean standards of elegance and wit, and every Sunday during term presided over a salon in his rooms in Beaumont Street.

Sadly, the tone was often lowered by the childish behaviour of his guests, but Kolkhurst persevered. He wore a lump of sugar around his neck 'to sweeten the conversation'. He dressed in a suit of white flannel, including a white flannel waistcoat. He carried an ear trumpet, the better to hear clever remarks, and ostentatiously put it away when he was bored. He developed a refined technique for reprimanding those who had displeased him: on their next visit the offenders were given a glass of the dreaded marsala, instead of the sherry offered to those in favour. Those who neglected to address Kolkhurst by his nickname were liable to incur this penalty. Known ironically as 'The Colonel' because of his studiously languid air, Kolkhurst, who had never been in the army, was at first puzzled by the title; in time, according to Osbert Lancaster, he came to insist upon its use.

Although he had had a distinguished career as a student and enjoyed a reputation as a gifted, if unorthodox teacher, it was Kolkhurst's innocent determination to construct his life according to a romantic image of the past, rather than his scholarship, that endeared him to several generations of amused undergraduates.

107

Langford
Mr

angford's will was a refinement of the traditional English document in which the deceased's fortune is left to his or her favourite pet. Langford's dog was, of course, left a comfortable income and his executors charged with seeing that Fido was well cared for. But Langford, of Bolsover in Derbyshire, also directed that the dog be provided with a sable mantle and that he lead the way as chief mourner at the funeral, with the family following, as they were no doubt accustomed to do, several paces behind.

'The Hermit of Newton-Burgoland'

Lole
William

Although William Lole called himself a hermit, his character seems to have been anything but retiring. Observing that 'true hermits throughout every age, have been the firm abettors of freedom', he went to unusual lengths to proclaim his own ideas on religion and political liberty. All his clothes were symbolic of something. His hats, each with its own story to tell, were numbered, named, and emblazoned with mottoes and emblems. Number 17, for example, was called 'Wash Basin of Reform' and had the legend, 'white-washed face and blackened heart'. Lole's hat wardrobe also included: number 5, 'Bellows', 'Blow the flames of freedom with God's word of truth'; number 15, 'Patent Teapot', 'To draw out the flavour of the tea best – Union and Goodwill'; and number 20, 'Beehive', 'The toils of industry are sweet, a wise people live at peace.'

Lole had twelve suits, also named and decorated with symbols. Odd Fellows was a long, loose robe of white linen, girdled at the waist with a white belt, and adorned with a heart-shaped badge called the 'Order of the Star'. His military dress, for special occasions only, was like an old-fashioned uniform, but the cocked hat had two protuberances on either side resembling horses' ears.

Lole's passion for symbolism extended to the garden of his home in Newton-Burgoland near Ashby-de-la-Zouch, Leicestershire. Entrance was effected via a passage containing 'the three seats of Self-Inquiry' which asked, 'Am I vile?', 'Am I a hypocrite?'; 'Am I a Christian?' A ramble round the garden provided more food for thought: arrangements of different coloured flowers or pebbles spelt out patriotic sentiments such as 'God save our Noble Queen' and 'Britons never shall be Slaves'.

Lole was a champion of religious and political freedom. He had flower-covered mounds in his garden which he titled 'Graves of the Reformers', along with effigies of the apostles and tableaux of the Inquisition and Purgatory. When visitors came, as they frequently did, he climbed into a large tub – his pulpit – and preached against Popery and oppression. This was not a profitable occupation, but, happily, Lole was able to survive through the bounty and goodwill of his neighbours.

Earl of Lonsdale

Lowther
Sir James

James Lowther, Earl of Lonsdale, was known as 'the bad earl'. Carlyle said that he was 'more detested than any man alive as a shameless political sharper . . . and an intolerable tyrant over his tenants and dependants.' He controlled nine seats in Parliament, and contemporary satirists, who found in his political intriguing a wealth of material, called him 'Jemmy Graspall, Earl of Toadstool'. Lowther's sponsorship of Pitt in 1781 in one of his safe seats earned him a peerage three years later, but the manner of its bestowal caused some problems. Lowther, a baronet by birth, was raised directly to an Earldom, skipping the stages of Baron and Viscount in the peerage. Elevated with him were two barons, scions of ancient families, who would naturally take precedence over a baronet. When the list was published Lowther was furious to see his name last. He attempted to forswear his title and had to be forcibly restrained by the Serjeant-at-Arms from resuming his seat in the Commons. Later, when tempers had cooled, Lowther, now Lonsdale, was prevailed upon to forgive the hapless Pitt, who demonstrated his gratitude for such generosity of spirit by heaping yet more honours up on the shoulders of his demanding mentor.

Lonsdale, one imagines, was not the most affectionate of characters; indeed his wife does not loom large in accounts of his career. He did, however, fall desperately in love with the daughter of one of his tenant farmers. He persuaded her to run off with him and they stayed together until her death at an early age. Heartbroken and unaccustomed to having his wishes thwarted, even by death, Lonsdale decided to keep her with him. He had her embalmed and kept her in a glass-topped coffin in his home, Maulds Meaburn Hall, in Westmoreland.

Money was Lonsdale's other great love and that affair was longer lasting. After he died it was discovered that Lowther collected guineas. There were 16,000 guineas in his house, neatly sorted into bags of 500 coins apiece. Each bag was labelled according to the quality of the coins it contained – indifferent, very perfect or super excellent.

Most of his £100,000 annual income was spent buying influence and waging political battles. Very little went on keeping up the appearances due to his rank. Lowther felt that he was above such petty displays and enjoyed demonstrating his contempt for public opinion by going around in a rusty carriage with untrimmed horses. Instead of deer in a well-kept park, Lowther had wild horses in his overgrown and uncared-for garden. He lived in the burnt-out shell of Lowther Hall, a magnificent Queen Anne house that had been nearly destroyed by an accidental fire in 1720, and which he had not bothered to rebuild.

Lonsdale's tenants and creditors followed his example of austerity out of necessity rather than admiration. Lonsdale was never, by any stretch of the imagination, a generous landlord, and for a period he declined to settle with any of his creditors. He owed a great deal of money to Wordsworth's father, whose five children inherited nothing but bills due upon Lonsdale – bills which were unhonoured during the Earl's lifetime. His rationale for this piece of miserliness was ingenious: if those to whom he owed money were near neighbours, Lowther 'knew them to be knaves'; if they were strangers, 'how could he know what they were?'

Lucas
James

As a boy James Lucas was petted and indulged by his mother. He sometimes took a whim to stay in bed for days on end, hoarding the plates on which his meals were sent up to him. When he went out driving with his sisters, he dressed extravagantly, often wore his hair in curl-papers, and kept his eyes closed. On his walks about the neighbourhood of Hitchin, Lucas, carrying a green parasol, was followed at five paces by a manservant.

These were but youthful peculiarities, however. It was the death of his mother in 1849 that turned this intelligent and well-read man into a remarkable eccentric. James had always been close to his mother, but after an unrequited love affair with Isabella Amos, a local beauty, he devoted himself entirely to her. When Mrs Lucas died, James embalmed her himself and kept her by him for three months, refusing to allow the local authorities to bury her. Finally, the police intervened and removed Mrs Lucas to the churchyard. From that time on Lucas became a confirmed recluse.

He barricaded himself in the family house at Great Wymondley, Hertfordshire, and settled down to live in the kitchen. There was no furniture in his 'cell', but he kept a fire going night and day and slept on a bed of ashes. These were never removed, and by the time of his death the ashes, packed down though they had been over twenty-five years, reached to more than half the height of the room.

Lucas never washed, and neither combed nor cut his hair. He wore nothing but a blanket fastened with a skewer, and used a piece of broken glass as a monocle. His clothes never changed, though he ordered a new white blanket and a white beaver hat when he went into mourning for his horse, Junie. His diet consisted of bread, cheese, eggs, red herrings and gin, which he kept in a basket hung from the ceiling in an attempt to foil the rats he had encouraged as pets.

Lucas received many visitors at the barred windows of his kitchen-cell, but he had little time for rich business men, lawyers and those who merely regarded him as a freak One impertinent woman was rebuffed with a withering look through his monocle and the haughty remark: 'A little of the

coolie class I should say.' On another occasion, he used a rusty shotgun to rout a whole platoon of Dragoon officers who had stormed the house in an effort to get a good look at him.

He was, however, very far from being a misanthropist. He enjoyed the company of tramps, vagabonds and scholars. Every Good Friday he gave a party for children. Two hundred youngsters came to the last of these, each of whom received from the hermit through the bars of his cell one penny, a bun, some sweets and a glass of gin and water. For his educated visitors, Lucas kept a special supply of sherry. Most found him gracious, well-informed and alert, though Dickens took an instant and rather unfair dislike to him and parodied him in 'All the Year Round' as Mr Mopes, an 'obscure nuisance'. Lucas had also arranged a standing order with his bank to provide him with £25-worth of coins each month which he gave away to needy callers, along with liberal quantities of gin. At the end of his life, he estimated that he had helped fifteen to twenty thousand tramps. These included a large number of instant converts to Roman Catholicism as Lucas, whose mother had been a Catholic, was especially generous to those who knew their Paternosters.

As an ardent Jacobite, he refused to recognise Queen Victoria or Parliament, and would not accept anything bearing the royal stamp, including paper money. This conscientious stance cost Lucas a considerable amount, because it meant that he could not collect monies owed him by tenants and other creditors.

Lucas's bizarre way of life inevitably laid him open to charges of insanity, but when the Commissioners of Lunacy examined him in 1851, they declared that 'so far from being insane, the Hermit was a man of the most acute intelligence'.

Lucas died in 1874 of an apoplectic fit. The house was by then a crumbling ruin. Seventeen cartloads of ash were removed from his room and a family of foxes was found to be living in one wing of the dilapidated mansion.

McGonagall
William

cGonagall's first venture into the arts was as an actor. In 1872 he paid £1 to the manager of a local theatre in Dundee for the privilege of taking the leading role in *Macbeth*. McGonagall's mates at the hand-loom mill where he worked were apparently connoisseurs of the theatre – or of McGonagall – for his debut appearance was standing-room only. He describes the triumph in his 'Brief Autobiography'. 'The applause was deafening and was continued through the entire evening. . . . The house was crowded during each of the three performances on that ever-memorable night which can never be forgot by me or my shop-mates and even entire strangers included. . . . What a sight it was to see such a mass of people struggling to gain admission! hundreds failing to do so, and in the struggle numbers were trapped under foot. . . . So much then for the true account of my first appearance on any stage.'

So carried away was McGonagall with the glory of imper-sonating the Scottish king that at his next performance he refused to be slain. In an unrehearsed departure from the script Macbeth continued to flourish his sword for some time after being run through by Macduff; he was only finally brought to the ground by a well-placed kick from the actor playing Macduff who had lost his temper at this improvisation. The audience, of course, loved it.

Five years later, however, McGonagall's life was to take a new turn when he discovered to his great surprise that he was a poet. Sitting in his room one June day in 1877, 'I imagined that a pen was in my right hand and a voice crying, 'Write, Write!' So I said to myself, ruminating, Let me see; what shall I write?' The answer came quickly: a poem about his friend the Rev. George Gilfillan. From this poem, which appeared soon thereafter in the *Dundee Weekly News*, I quote the first two verses, which demonstrate that the poet had hit immediately upon the distinc-tive style that was to remain his trademark.

Rev George Gilfillan of Dundee,
There is none can you excel;
You have boldly rejected the Confession of Faith,
And defended your cause right well.

The first time I heard him speak,
'Twas in the Kinnaird hall,
Lecturing on the Garibaldi movement,
As loud as he could bawl.

To celebrate his newly discovered gift, McGonagall had cards made reading 'William McGonagall, Poet and Tragedian'. Henceforth he devoted himself to his poetic muse. McGonagall was both prolific and ambitious and he soon penned a 'Requisition to the Queen', asking her to accept two other poems. So heartened was he by the response, which took the form of a letter from Lord Biddulph saying that Her Majesty could not possibly accept the verse, that he began styling himself 'Poet to Her Majesty' and planned a journey to see his patroness at Balmoral.

The trip, which McGonagall terms 'my far-famed Balmoral journey', was something of a disappointment since he was turned away at the porter's lodge. To support his request for an interview, McGonagall gave the porter the letter of patronage – which he always carried in his breast pocket – but to no avail: 'I've been up to the Castle with your letter,' the porter later informed him, 'and the answer is they cannot be bothered with you.'

McGonagall now supported himself and his family by giving readings in public places; by printing and selling his poems; and occasionally by resorting to his old trade of weaving, for he was chronically short of money. In this respect at least he was a true poet. However, with his poetry and news of his performances regularly finding their way into the local press, he was making a name for himself.

McGonagall, conscious of his responsibility to be seen to be a poet, always dressed in accordance with his view of that role. He kept his hair long, a peculiarity to which the citizens of Dundee never adjusted; wore a wide-brimmed hat and a long coat over his shabby clothes, summer and winter; and carried a walking stick. This last item was also useful as a prop in one of his most-requested recitations, 'The Rattling Boy from Dublin Town', a piece with a strong temperance moral. McGonagall's fervent support of this cause often excited violent feelings in the inns and pubs where he gave most of his readings. 'The first man who threw peas at me', he tells us, 'was a publican.' Well might McGonagall remember this incident for it became almost a tradition to express contempt for the aims of the temperance movement by throwing food at its leading poet. McGonagall even worked up a verse in response to this: 'Gentlemen if you please/Stop throwing peas.'

Part of McGonagall's popularity and fame, such as it was, undoubtedly stemmed from a desire on the part of the public to make fun of him, but though he was aware of such an element among his audiences he regarded it as beneath contempt and paid no attention to it. McGonagall preferred to look on the bright side and, after all, he did have his triumphs. He travelled to America (a voyage of 'twelve days – of course nights included as well'). His stay in the New World was brief, for work was hard to find, but in 1801 McGonagall received further royal encouragement in a letter from Sir Henry Ponsonby thanking him on the Queen's behalf for a poem called 'The Royal Review' and regretting that she could not accept it. Three years later McGonagall received a letter from the Court of King Theebaw, Andaman Islands, appointing him a Grand Knight of the Holy Order of the White Elephant, Burmah, and entitling him to sign his name – as he did henceforth – Sir William Topaz McGonagall, GKHOWEB. There was also the hope of succeeding Tennyson as Poet Laureate, a post which McGonagall felt strongly had gone to someone with more influence than talent.

His first volume of poems, with 100 subscribers, appeared in 1890 and sold well at 1 shilling a copy. He had notable successes at readings to literary clubs in Inverness, Perth and Glasgow, some founded specifically for the purpose of inviting McGonagall as guest speaker. A number of these occasions were commemorated in verse, showing the poet's fine eye for detail:

The Banquet consisted of roast beef, potatoes, and red wine,
Also hare soup and sherry, and grapes most fine,
And baked pudding and apples, lovely to be seen,
Also rich sweet milk and delicious cream.

When his second volume of poetry did not fare as well as the first, McGonagall thought of the advantages to be gained by mentioning commercial products in his poems and discovered, luckily, that his Muse was not at all adverse to this idea. The makers of Sunlight Soap paid two guineas for the following:

You can use it with great pleasure and ease
Without wasting any elbow grease;
And when washing the most dirty clothes
The sweat won't be dripping from your nose.

This effort was followed up with,

Gentlemen you have my best wishes, and I hope
That the poem I've written about Sunlight Soap
Will cause a demand for it in every clime,
For I declare it to be superfine.
And I hope before long without any joke,
You will require some more of my poems about Sunlight
*   Soap.*
And in conclusion, gentlemen, I thank ye –
William McGonagall, Poet, 48 Step Row, Dundee.

McGonagall continued to write poetry to the very end of his life, but his popularity waned and he died in poverty. His last poem, on the Coronation of Edward VII – written only weeks before his death of a cerebral haemorrhage in September 1902 – contains some of his most creative rhymes, for example:

Then robed in purple and velvet,
They prepare to take their departure,
The Queen goes first and the King follows after.

Maguire
Brian

Brian Maguire, a scion of the ancient and once powerful house of Fermanagh, was an officer in the East India Company, which he joined in 1799. His first duel took place while on duty at Cochin, a seaport on the Malabar Coast where one Captain Thuring took objection to Maguire's success with the very limited supply of ladies and found a pretext to challenge him.

The match was somewhat unequal since Maguire faced the Captain's sword with only a billiard cue. However, he escaped unscathed, and Thuring was fatally wounded. Having thus cleared his name, Maguire found that there was no turning back; he became addicted to the art of duelling. His return to Dublin and marriage in 1808 in no way cramped his style. Indeed, his wife, who might have been a pacific influence on him, instead assisted him by holding – at arm's length – the lighted candle he used for target practice.

A shortage of opponents was Maguire's greatest difficulty but the resourceful Irishman solved this problem by hanging out of the window and throwing dirt on passers-by. When they looked up, he spat on them and immediately offered them the opportunity of settling the matter on the field of honour.

A long and ultimately unsuccessful Chancery suit for recovery of his wife's fortune led to Maguire's eventual impoverishment. When his eldest son, George, died at the age of twelve in 1830, Maguire, using techniques he had acquired during his time in the East, embalmed him himself. He kept George in a glass case, always by his side, up to the moment of his own death, five years later.

Mathew
George

For seven years George Mathew exiled himself to the Continent, saving up his money to turn his home, Thomastown Castle, into a pleasure garden for his friends. The extensive grounds were completely landscaped – the first in Ireland to be laid out in the new natural style. Inside he created forty private apartments in which his guests could live as they pleased, for as long as they pleased. Each room was beautifully furnished, with every convenience provided. Although there were rooms for visitors' servants, Mathew's own large staff included an attendant for each guest. He also laid down a law that servants were not to be tipped, as he felt it was inhospitable to put guests to even a small expense; instead Mathew himself added the equivalent of a generous tip to the servants' regular wages.

Once at Thomastown, in County Tipperary, a guest had merely to express his wishes to find them obeyed. There was only one house rule: visitors were asked never to acknowledge Mathew as the owner and host, but simply to treat him as a fellow-guest. Shortly after a new arrival was shown to his room, the cook knocked at the door to receive instructions for dinner. He was followed by the butler with a list of wines and liquors from which the guest was asked to select as many as he wanted.

One was free to have any or all meals in one's own room alone or with friends, or to join those dining downstairs. Mathew was usually amongst the latter but he never sat at the head of the table.

For those who preferred it, Mathew had recreated a Dublin coffee-house at Thomastown where food was available at all hours and visitors might sit and argue, play chess or back-gammon, or read the lastest newspapers and magazines. Other guests spent their mornings in the tavern. Here one might while away time playing cards or billiards; waiters took orders for food and drink. Like the coffee-house, the tavern was furnished and run with complete authenticity, with the one exception that betting was not allowed: Mathew wanted his guests to enjoy, not to ruin, themselves.

Outdoorsmen could look forward to fishing, shooting or hunting in Mathew's several thousand acres. He, of course, pro-vided the necessary equipment from a large supply of fishing tackle, numerous guns, twenty excellent hunters and several packs of foxhounds, stag hounds and harriers.

The lucky objects of all this pampering were not brilliant celebrities imported to gratify Mathew's ego, but ordinary members of the squirarchy: friends from school, relatives, neighbours. Although one guest said he always appeared the most disengaged man in the house, Mathew himself worked very hard to keep things running efficiently. He rose at an early hour every morning to go over the books, consult with his staff and deal with each day's problems. Thomastown Castle was, in effect, a hotel for his friends; Mathew, the unpaid but devoted manager. By prudent planning and rigorous behind-the-scenes organisation, Mathew was able to entertain his friends, improve Thomastown, and hand on his fortune intact to his heir.

One famous visitor to Thomastown was Dean Swift. In 1719, Swift, not always the most sociable of men, was invited to stay a fortnight by Sheridan, who knew Mathew. When he saw the size of the Castle and realised that there would be many other guests, Swift was all for turning back and only reluctantly gave in to Sheridan's pleading, saying, 'Well, there is no remedy, I must submit, but I have lost a fortnight of my life.'

Swift was sceptical when he was greeted, as all Mathew's

guests were, with the words, 'This is your castle. Here you are to command as absolutely as in your own home.' The appearance at his door of the cook and butler softened him somewhat, but he still elected to eat alone in his room and avoid his fellow guests.

After four days of remaining aloof, during which time to his astonishment no one tried to draw him out, Swift was tempted downstairs by hearing the laughter of the party in the dining room. He came to dinner saying, 'And now Ladies and Gentlemen, I am come to live among you and it will be no fault of mine if we do not pass our time pleasantly.' After this surrender Swift, who proceeded to entertain the entire company, clearly enjoyed himself greatly for he extended his stay at Thomastown from two weeks to four months.

Matthewson
R. N.

In 1912, Mr R N Matthewson of Swan Park, Alipore, Calcutta, collected his new car from the makers in Lowestoft, Sussex. The car was shaped like a swan and had a Gabriel horn with eight organ pipes and a keyboard which worked off the exhaust system. The swan's beak opened by a lever. A second lever sent half a pint of hot water from the radiator into the swan's nostrils. This was forced out by compressed air, making an authentically swan-like hissing sound.

Mr Matthewson, well pleased with his swan car, took it back with him to India, where it was as great a success as it had been on the roads of England. Unfortunately, it caused such crowds to gather that the police were forced eventually to ban the swan car from the streets of Calcutta.

Maturin
Charles Robert

Maturin was an Irish clergyman who wrote plays and novels, notably *Melmoth the Wanderer*, a masterpiece of the gothic style. The patronage of Byron and Sir Walter Scott helped him achieve a certain literary recognition, but it did not free him of his perpetual financial difficulties, which were largely the result of an act of kindness in standing security for a bankrupt relative.

When Maturin did get a bit of money, however, he spent it flamboyantly. The ceiling of his house in Dublin was painted with clouds, and scenes from his novels were reproduced on the walls.

It was Maturin's joy to see his wife, who was a great beauty, well turned out, but he also insisted on her wearing layers of rouge and more than once ordered her back to her dressing table for a thicker application. Maturin's own dress was dictated by a desire to show off his fine figure to good effect. He favoured a huge greatcoat tossed gracefully over his shoulders and tight pantaloons to display his legs. He wore net stockings and evening clothes even when fishing.

Maturin loved music; he had a good voice and claimed to be 'the best dancer in the Established Church'. In Dublin he held quadrille parties several mornings a week. Morning, noon and night were all one to him: the sun never penetrated his perpetually closed shutters and he lived by artificial light.

Maturin liked to be surrounded by people while he was working. When he was under the influence of the muse, he would stick a wafer on his head as a signal that he should not be disturbed. At other times, conversation could go on as usual around him and he merely ensured that he should not take part by covering his mouth with a paste made of bread and water.

He was tremendously absent-minded, sometimes even in matters that he cared deeply about, such as dress. He often made social calls in his dressing gown and slippers or went out wearing one boot and one shoe. He loved parties, but was likely to turn up a day early or late. And he sent his great novel, *Melmoth*, to his publishers as a stack of several thousand out-of-order, unnumbered pages.

Mytton
John

John Mytton was a sporting man. At the age of twelve he prevailed upon his widowed mother to allow him to establish his own pack of harriers. He was also high spirited, strong willed and used to having his own way. Mrs Mytton, unable to cope, depended upon the good influence of John's tutor, a tractable cleric named William Owen.

Luckily Owen, a keen outdoorsman himself, was able to accept being the victim of his charge's numerous practical jokes. On one occasion he spent the night with a pony that young Jack had coaxed up the stairs and into Owen's bedroom, and that refused to budge from there until morning.

Eventually the private tutorials came to an end. In 1807 at the age of eleven, Mytton was sent to Westminster School, where, as a contemporary remembered, 'the boys fought one another; they fought the Masters; the Masters fought them; they fought outsiders; in short we were ready to fight anybody.' After a year Mytton proved too pugnacious even for this set: he was expelled, sent to Harrow, and after only four days, was thrown out of that establishment as well.

Owen came once more into Mytton's life when he advised his erstwhile pupil to go to University: 'Upon my word, sir, you must go. Every man of fortune ought to go to Christ Church if only for a term or so.' Mytton's reaction was sullen. 'Well then, if I do go, I go on the following terms – that I never open a book!' 'There is not the least occasion to – not the smallest', was Owen's reassuring reply. It appears that Mytton had settled on Cambridge, as he ordered more than 2,000 bottles of port to be sent up in anticipation of his arrival, but at the last moment he thought better of it and embarked upon the Grand Tour instead.

In 1816, after his return from the Continent, he joined the 7th Hussars, and spent a pleasant year gambling, drinking, and racing with the army of occupation in France. With his majority approaching Mytton decided to leave the army and return to take charge of the family estates at Halston, in Shropshire. His last gesture as a soldier was to jump his old one-eyed horse, Baronet, right over the fully laden messtable as a farewell salute to his fellow officers.

Mytton came into a fortune of £60,000 in cash and estates

worth £18,000 a year. He needed all this, and more, for in the remaining seventeen years of his life he ran through more than £500,000. He began his adult life by running for Parliament. His appeal to voters was none too subtle: he walked the streets 'attired in a brilliant coloured coat trimmed with gold buttons and a ten pound note, intended for voters to snatch at, attached to each button.' These notes were replaced as they were taken, so that altogether Mytton spent £10,000 to win his place in Parliament. One might wonder why he bothered since, having made a half-hour appearance for his swearing in, Mytton returned to Halston and never showed himself at Westminster again.

Meanwhile his fame as a daredevil sportsman and practical joker spread. Not content with riding fifty miles or more to and from meets several times a week, Mytton enjoyed going at fences, ditches, and streams in a gig or a tandem. One night while dining with friends he agreed, on a wager of £150, to drive his tandem from the house to the highway – straight across a three-yard-wide sunk fence, a deep ditch and two hedges with ditches on the far side. The night was pitch black so twelve men were stationed along his route with lanterns. Mytton won the bet.

On another occasion he was driving his friend and biographer, Nimrod (C J Apperley), late at night when they found their way blocked by a high hedge and a ditch. Mytton took a look and cheerfully announced, 'We'll manage it. This horse is a capital fencer.' Nimrod got out and watched as Mytton – horse, carriage and all – cleared the hurdle.

Fear was a word Mytton refused to recognise. His impetuous style of riding and hunting led to numberless accidents and broken bones; indeed he often rode out with broken ribs or with his arm in a sling, but he scorned caution and expected others to do likewise. He was shocked to hear from a friend as they were out driving that he had never been upset in a gig. 'What?' cried Mytton. 'Never! What a damned slow fellow you must have been all your life!' He then deliberately overturned the gig they were in, just to rectify this outrageous state of affairs. Luckily – and Mytton was incredibly lucky – no one was hurt.

In his personal affairs Mytton was equally incautious. He started the day by opening a bottle of port which he drank as he shaved. Another four or five followed during the course of the day. Mytton was easily satisfied, however; he once drank a bottle of lavender water at his barber's when nothing else was available. How he managed to survive his field exploits with such a quantity of liquor under his belt is a mystery, but his drinking was such that a close friend signed an affidavit after Mytton's death to the effect that the Squire had been continually drunk for the previous twelve years.

If port was Mytton's drink, filberts were his food. He had a standing order with a shopkeeper in Shrewsbury for filberts and as many as two cartloads were delivered to Halston in a season. Once he and a friend shared a carriage from London to Halston with eighteen pounds of filberts and by the time they arrived they had eaten every one and were up to their knees in nut shells.

Mytton's taste in clothes ran to lightweight garments totally unsuited to the winter sports he loved. He often went out in the dead of winter bare-headed, wearing no gloves and no underwear, and clad only in the thinnest silk stockings, delicate shoes, an unbuttoned waistcoat, and unlined breeches. The better to camouflage himself while waiting in the snow for wild fowl, Mytton would often wear only a nightshirt, and once he crawled stark naked across a frozen pond in pursuit of some ducks. Still his wardrobe was immense, with 1000 hats, 3000 shirts and 152 pairs of breeches and trousers.

Mytton never lacked for animal companions: at one time Halston was home to 2000 dogs. He also had more than sixty cats, each dressed in a style that suited its own breed. Mytton had a way with animals and was supremely confident around them. He once intervened in a fight between two fierce seventy pound bulldogs, picking one dog up by the nose with his teeth and holding him suspended while the second was taken away to safety. He also had a pet bear named Nell, which was docile enough with him, but not so reliable with other people. There was havoc after one of Mytton's dinner parties when the host appeared in the dining-room in full hunting pink, mounted on Nell. In the excitement – with his friends jumping out of the windows and leaping onto the furniture – Mytton forgot himself and calling out Tally-ho, spurred his unbroken mount, who retaliated by sinking her teeth into his leg. Nell was finally removed, and Mytton's leg eventually healed, sooner no doubt than did his guests' nerves.

Bringing animals into the house had been a fancy of Mytton's ever since his prank with the pony at the age of nine. In later years he sometimes sat his favourite horse, Baronet, by the fire after a hard day's hunting and served him mulled port.

Friends and neighbours were kept alert, if not always

amused, by Mytton's exploits. These included setting four foxes free in a public house in Shrewsbury; riding his horse upstairs into a hotel dining-room and jumping, still on horseback, from the balcony down into the street; buttering a piece of bread, topping it with a five pound note and eating it; and replacing the last few pages of Mr Owen's – now Mytton's own chaplain – sermon with pages from the *Sporting Magazine*.

On one occasion Mytton got George Underhill, his horse-dealer, drunk and put him into bed with two bulldogs and Nell. Another time, Mytton gave Underhill a note to a banker in Shrewsbury, ostensibly authorising him to collect money on Mytton's behalf. Instead the banker, who was also a Governor of the local Lunatic Asylum, read this message: 'Sir, admit the bearer, George Underhill, to the Lunatic Asylum. Your Obedient Servant, John Mytton.'

On other occasions, Mytton amused himself by dressing up as a highwayman and robbing his own dinner guests at gunpoint or holding up his butler for the household payroll. Posing as a trespasser on his own property, Mytton was once thrashed by an applicant for the post of keeper on the estate. He cast off his disguise and hired the man on the spot.

In spite of his impetuous, and often dangerous, behaviour, Mytton's generosity made him popular with his tenants. He gave money away as freely as he spent it. Visitors to Halston were likely to find bundles of notes lying around the grounds where their host had dropped them. One man, at whose parents' inn Mytton often stopped, recalled, 'My dear mother has often told me that nothing delighted him more than to fill my little fist with silver, which was to be all my own if I cursed and swore like a trooper.'

Mytton's first wife died in 1820 after two years of marriage; he remarried, but the second Mrs Mytton left her husband in 1830. He was fond of both his wives, but was totally unfit for marriage and certainly left a great deal to be desired as a husband. At about the time of his separation from Caroline, his second wife, Mytton's financial difficulties began to get very serious. His friends had long advised him that his spending was over the mark, but Mytton could never take advice, saying, 'What the devil is the use of my having a head on my own shoulders if I am obliged to make use of yours?'

Mytton hardly knew what he owed since he made a habit of never opening any letters, except those on which he recognised the handwriting. All others he assumed to be bills and sent straight on to his agent. Nimrod tried to counsel Mytton, telling him that if he would only live on £6,000 a year he would be saved. Mytton's response was a blank refusal: 'I would not give a straw for life if it was to be passed on £6,000 a year.' He talked of selling Halston and when reminded by anxious relatives that it had been in the family for 500 years he said, 'The devil it has! Then it is high time it should go out of it.'

Eventually Mytton made his way to Calais to escape the bailiffs. Even in exile he had a few Myttonesque tricks up his sleeve. One evening in his hotel, impatient with a persistent attack of hiccups, he picked up a lighted candle, saying, 'Damn this hiccup! I'll frighten it away!', and set fire to his night-clothes. Luckily two companions were able to tear off the flaming nightshirt, but Mytton was horribly burned. As he collapsed onto his bed he cried, 'The hiccup is gone, by God!'

This foolish act of bravado, which owed something to the effects of brandy, kept Mytton in bed for four months. Of course, he found the notion of an enforced rest intolerable and the very day after the incident he insisted on dining out with a friend. A month later he announced his intention of paying a call on Nimrod. Knowing that, although he disapproved of the idea, he couldn't stop Mytton, Nimrod ordered a carriage to fetch his friend from the hotel. When Mytton, still swathed in bandages, saw a measly two-horse equipage at his door, he was furious and said he would sooner walk than settle for less than four horses. And walk he did, though it took two men to support him.

At the end of 1832 he returned to England to sign some papers and was briefly confined in the King's Bench. On his release Mytton was walking across Westminster Bridge when he saw an attractive young woman. He asked where she was going. 'I don't know', was the reply. 'Well, then,' he said, 'come live with me and I will settle £500 a year on you.' The girl, whose name was Susan, agreed and they went off to Calais together. Mytton was quite in love and Susan proved to be a very kind and sympathetic creature. After further adventures, mainly concerned with repeated arrests and imprisonments for small debts, Mytton, who by this time was ill from over-indulgence in drink, was fetched back to England by his mother. In early 1834 he was again confined in the King's Bench Prison where he died, from *delirium tremens*, at the end of March 1834.

Three thousand people attended Mytton's coffin to its burial in a field behind the family chapel at Halston.

Neild
James Camden

eild, a barrister, succceeded in 1814 at the age of thirty-four to an estate worth £250,000. His father had been a prison-reformer and philanthropist, but the son preferred to hoard money rather than to give it away. He practised all the usual miserly virtues: sleeping on a bare board in a sparsely furnished house; prolonging the life of his clothes by refusing to have them cleaned or brushed; walking all the way from his home in Chelsea to inspect his Buckinghamshire estates; staying in his tenant farmers' rough hovels to save the cost of a night's lodging. At the same time Neild had one very unmiserly quirk. He disliked getting anything for free and always insisted on paying a pittance (never more if he could help it) for favours given.

It was Neild's responsibility to keep the church at North Marston, Berkshire, where he had property, in good repair. When the time came to renew the roof of the chancel he instructed his workmen to re-cover it not with lead but with strips of calico, assuring everyone that they would 'last my time'. To make certain that his men put in a good day's work, Neild sat on the pitched roof watching them until the job was finished.

Thanks to his parsimony, Neild was able to double his fortune by the time he died. He clearly thought it right and proper that the rich get richer, for, making no mention of the housekeeper who had served him faithfully for twenty-six years, Neild in his will left his entire fortune – £500,000 – to Queen Victoria, 'begging her Majesty's most gracious acceptance of the same for her sole use and benefit'.

The Queen did graciously accept the bequest and in 1855 she used it to redo the calico-roofed chancel of Neild's North Marston church.

Noailles
Helena Comtesse de

The Comtesse de Noailles devoted her life to supporting the arts and staving off infection, not necessarily in that order. The daughter of a wealthy English family (her mother was a Baring, half-sister to Lord Revelstoke and Lord Cromer), Helena married Antonin, the Comte de Noailles, in 1849. After three years the couple decided to live apart and the Comtesse, always known as Madame, was free to follow her own whims.

The most remarkable result of her interest in art was her decision to buy a beautiful nine-year-old Spanish girl whose father had brought her to Paris as an artist's model. In 1865 Madame gave Maria Pasqua's father two bags of gold and assumed responsibility for the child's upbringing. Her lack of experience in raising children did not prevent her from holding very strong views on the subject.

Maria was sent to an English convent school at St Leonards, Sussex, but Madame insisted on certain conditions being observed. The school pond, which she considered a dangerous breeding ground for insects, had to be drained. Maria was only permitted milk from a cow that Madame had chosen and approved. Madame considered the ordinary school uniform restrictive, so Maria wore a loose Grecian tunic and open sandals. Instead of following the standard curriculum, Maria was to be taught grammar and arithmetic according to an improved system that Madame herself had devised.

Madame was an ardent phrenologist, firmly believing that the shape of the head is the key to a person's character. She had plans to turn one of her houses into a home for orphaned daughters of Church of England clergymen – admission to be determined on the basis of an examination by two qualified phrenologists. There were to be no competitive exams; no study after 6 p.m.; no arithmetic for children under ten; and no vaccinations. In many respects Madame la Comtesse had very advanced ideas about health and education. Her abhorrence of restrictive clothing; advocacy of fresh air; and objections to undue academic pressure on young children are attitudes with which most people today would agree.

Some of her ideas, however, or her single-mindedness in putting them into practice, seem as odd now as they did then. When

129

at teatime one day Maria's son, Phil, took his bun and climbed up into a tree to eat it, Madame decided that he had unconsciously proved Darwin's views about the descent of man. Thereafter, the child was expected to take his tea in the trees every day.

Madame's health regimen was strict. She went to bed every night with stockings filled with grey squirrel fur wrapped around her forehead and chin; and a wildcat skin, imported from Norway, covering her chest. Her cure for bronchitis was a diet of soft herring roe. Blue silk covers were made for all the brass door handles in her house in order to cut down on glare. For the same purpose the windows were furnished with green curtains and red glass – an unfortunate colour combination if the object was to lessen eyestrain.

Madame was a keen believer in the benefits of fresh air and methane gas; she was careful to keep a number of cows tethered near her windows so that she could enjoy the salutary effects of their exhalations. At mealtimes she took her food behind a two-foot high screen set up around her plate. No one was quite sure if modesty was her motive or if special food was served behind the screen.

Travelling, for someone with the Comtesse's high standards, was not a simple matter. First of all, no trip could be undertaken in an east wind and she did not scruple to stop a train if weather conditions were not to her liking. She travelled in private railway cars, the object being to avoid contact with the other, possibly infectious, travellers. For Channel crossings she had a specially wide carriage, formerly the property of King Louis Philippe. Upholstered in damask throughout, it contained a folding-bed, a portable lavatory, storage space for her luggage and enough food to last the journey. This was driven straight onto the Channel steamer and off at the other side, making it unnecessary for Madame ever to alight and run the risk of catching something nasty from the other first-class passengers. Once at the hotel, she demanded the best room and insisted that a string of onions be hung outside the door to ward off infection.

In 1881 Maria married an Englishman named Phillip Shepheard and settled in Norfolk. When Madame decided to visit them, she asked only that they prepare for her arrival by cutting down all the trees in the vicinity of the house, and bringing the cows into the garden to improve the atmosphere.

Madame's concern for Maria's health did not cease with her marriage. Her advice during one pregnancy was to drink only water in which pine tree-tops had been boiled. Madame ensured that her advice would be followed even after her death by making Maria's inheritance conditional on her wearing white in summer and eschewing laced shoes.

She lived to the age of eighty-four, existing at the end on champagne and milk, and left £100,000 and eleven wills for her heirs to sort out.

'Emperor of the United States'
Norton
Joshua

Joshua Norton reigned as Emperor of the United States and Protector of Mexico for over twenty years until his death in 1880. Born in London in 1819, he built up a considerable fortune in South Africa and San Francisco dealing in foodstuffs and property. In 1853 Norton saw his chance to hit it really big by cornering the rice market. He bought and held all available rice; as prices soared he foresaw enormous profits. His castles in Spain crumbled, however, when several ships laden with rice sailed into San Francisco Bay. The market was glutted, prices dropped and Norton lost everything. In 1856 he filed for bankruptcy.

Within a year he had confided to several friends that he was actually Norton I, Emperor of California. However, in 1859 he decided that the State of California did not have the authority to name him Emperor and that, in order for his title to be legitimate, he would have to be Emperor of all the United States. Accordingly, he handed the following proclamation to the editor of the *San Francisco Bulletin*, who printed it without comment.

At the pre-emptory request and desire of a large majority of the citizens of the United States, I, Joshua A Norton, . . . declare and proclaim myself Emperor of the US and in virtue of the authority thereby in me vested, do hereby order and direct the representatives of the different States of the Union to assemble in Musical Hall, of this city, on the last day of February next, then and there to make such alteration in the existing laws of the

Union as may ameliorate the evils under which the country is labouring, and thereby cause confidence to exist, both at home and abroad, in our stability and integrity.

Norton I Emperor of the United States
17 September 1859

Norton's chief concern at the beginning of his reign was the conflict between the States that was to lead to civil war. He felt that the United States needed a strong head of state to hold the country together and that the Presidency could not achieve this. Reluctantly, he dissolved the Republic, abolished Congress and the office of President and announced that he would henceforth rule personally. When this, like so many other of his Imperial decrees, was disregarded Norton was not shaken. At the outbreak of civil war he summoned both Lincoln and the rebel leader, Jefferson Davis, to his presence and issued a decree ordering hostilities to cease.

Emperor Norton took the responsibilities of his position seriously, mingling with his subjects each day as he strolled the streets of San Francisco inspecting construction sites, checking up on bus timetables and keeping in touch with the life of the city. His zeal to rule fairly even caused him to attend a different religious service every week so as to avoid giving rise to sectarian jealousy.

In response the citizens of San Francisco accepted his decrees with great good humour and respect, even acknowledging their responsibility to contribute to his upkeep. The Imperial Palace was only a small room in a seedy lodging house, but the 50 cent-a-night charge was paid by loyal subjects. Norton's wardrobe was a mixed bag of army and navy uniforms, outlandish hats and elaborate walking sticks. When it began to grow shabby he issued a decree: 'Know ye that we, Norton the First, have divers complaints from our liege subjects that our Imperial wardrobe is a national disgrace.' The following day the city council met and voted funds for a new uniform, to be supplied by the prestigious firm of Bullock and Jones, tailors by appointment to His Imperial Majesty. Norton's scrip (homemade 25 and 50 cent notes) was accepted freely by restaurateurs and shopkeepers; he had free passes to theatres and upon his entrance the audience always rose to their feet.

Once a river boat captain ordered Norton off his boat for not paying his fare. In retaliation Norton ordered the US Navy to blockade all the company's vessels. Hurriedly, the board of directors offered him an apology and a lifetime free pass.

Very rarely did the emperor use his power in a cruel way. One rather sad instance was his banishment of Uncle Freddie, a local character, who apparently took the Imperial decree seriously and left San Francisco, never to be seen again.

Norton occasionally journeyed to Sacramento, the State capital, to keep his eyes on the activities of the legislature. Once when the Assembly was deadlocked over an appointment, Norton spoke in favour of both men, but suggested that they appoint the only one of the two whom he knew personally. After a moment of shock, the bemused legislators unanimously complied with the Emperor's wish.

Like many public figures, Norton was subject to interference in his life by complete strangers. False telegrams were a favourite ploy and one wag attempted to arrange a marriage for Norton with the widowed Queen Victoria. Telegrams of congratulations on the proposed match purported to come from Tsar Alexander, Disraeli and Ulysses S. Grant.

Robert Louis Stevenson admired the people of San Francisco for fostering and encouraging this 'harmless madman'. They did so because Norton brought colour to their city and because, as a judge remarked, rebuking a policeman who had arrested Norton for lunacy, he had 'shed no blood, robbed no one and despoiled no country, which is more than can be said for most fellows in the king line'.

Ogden
Charles Kay

gden was a brilliant linguist, psychologist, philosopher and editor; he was also a bookseller, collector and critic (often under the pseudonym Adelyne More). None of his careers followed a conventional pattern, partly because everything Ogden did was wrapped in a veil of mystery. He never went to bed before dawn and often spent his nights strolling around London or Cambridge knocking up any friends whose lights were still on. He kept his wide and diverse circle of friends in different compartments and took it in very bad part if they got together without his permission, so no one really knew all sides of C.K.

Most people, however, knew he had a zany streak. At Cambridge he eschewed real cigarettes for a false one with a bulb at the end that glowed red. He always insisted that fresh air was harmful. He kept the windows in his flat closed and turned on something called an ozone machine which, he maintained, churned out a better grade of air than ordinary fresh and did him more good than a walk outside.

Towards the end of his life, Ogden kept his coffin handy in the front hall of his London house. He loved masks, of which he had a large collection, and advocated wearing them during arguments as a way of switching the emphasis away from personalities to issues.

Ogden collected everything. Books filled his room to overflowing – one visitor counted eighty-two family bibles – and were arranged, if at all, according to bizarre principles, such as the initial letters of the titles spelling out a word or phrase, the significance of which was often open to question. He also had quantities of music boxes, shoes (forty-two pairs by one count), clocks, and mechanical toys like the bird that sang only if asked to in Basic English.

Basic English was an invention of Ogden's – a simplified form of English designed for use as an international language, with a vocabulary of only 850 words. Churchill was an enthusiastic champion of Basic English during the Second World War, and the British Government gave it financial support until 1953.

Churchill's speech at Harvard in 1943 advocating the adoption of Basic as the international tongue gave a great boost to Ogden's cause. Yet when journalists came to interview him after the speech he confounded them by popping in and out of doors, each time wearing a new mask.

The difficulties faced by civil servants in dealing with such an individual can be imagined. One day the Chairman of the Cabinet Committee on Basic English tried to put through a call to Ogden in Buxton. The local operator, however, stoutly refused to connect him, even after he had explained who he was and that it was a Cabinet level matter. 'Mr Ogden told me you would say all that, Sir', she replied. 'He told me that if I gave you the number he would have a question about it raised in the House.' The feeling of frustration was evidently mutual, for Ogden's entry in *Who's Who* described his career as '1946–8, bedevilled by officials'.

Ogden was a great admirer of Jeremy Bentham, the nineteenth-century philosopher and reformer. One of Bentham's pet theories was that the bodies of dead people could be put to practical use. Every man, if properly embalmed, could serve as his own statue. Portraits of ancestors might be replaced by the heads themselves, 'many generations being deposited on a few shelves, in a moderate sized cupboard'. Very space-saving for a modest home, but if something grander was wanted, Bentham had an idea. 'If a country gentleman has rows of trees leading to his dwelling, the auto-icons of his family might alternate with the trees; copal varnish would protect the faces from the effects of rain.'

In line with this utilitarian philosophy, Bentham directed that his body first be dissected for the benefit of medical students and then be embalmed, dressed in his own clothes and placed in a glass case. His physician, Dr Southwood Smith, kept Bentham's body – with a wax head instead of the real thing, which had lost its expression during embalming – until he died in 1850. It was then given to University College, London, of which Bentham had been a governor. For many years the philosopher was present at meetings of the College Council; his only outing now is the annual Bentham dinner. It was at Ogden's suggestion that Bentham, after his first 100 years as an auto-icon, was cleaned up and given a change of underclothes.

Pockrich
Richard

ockrich ran through a fortune of £4,000 a year in a very short time, largely by failing at almost everything he tried. Among the expensive but impracticable schemes he dreamt up was a project to turn the Bishop of Tuam's residence outside Dublin into a tea house. This had to be dropped when the Bishop refused to move. Pockrich also planned to plant bogs with grapevines as the basis of an Irish wine-making industry. He proposed to give every Irishman a pair of wings, and promised: 'the means . . . to render this scheme feasible may be laid before the public at the proper time.' He hoped at one time to establish an observatory-cum-goose farm in the Wicklow mountains. Then there was his proposal for achieving eternal life by blood transfusions; with respect to this Pockrich realised that there might be complications if death were to vanish entirely from human experience, so he suggested an Act of Parliament to establish that anyone 'attaining to the age of 999 years, shall be deemed to all Intents and Purposes dead in law'. This would enable relatives to claim their inheritances and vicars to go to court to claim burial fees from legally dead 999-year-old parishioners.

Pockrich called himself 'perhaps the best master of harmony in the known world', so it is fitting that his only success was a musical instrument, called the Angelic Organ. Known more prosaically as musical glasses, this device consisted of a number of tumblers filled with varying amounts of water and 'played' by running a wetted finger around the rim.

Pockrich knew he was on to a good thing when two bailiffs who had come to arrest him for non-payment of taxes were so moved after a recital on the Angelic Organ that they couldn't bear to carry out their duty and left without making the arrest.

Unfortunately, the tour designed to bring Pockrich's invention to the attention of the civilised world got off to a bad start when, only three hours before the debut concert in Dublin, 'a large, unmannerly sow' made her way into the concert rooms and shattered most of the angelic glasses. However, the London debut in the following year, 1744, was a great success. Fame and fortune finally looked set to come Pockrich's way. Popular composers of the day wrote music especially for the musical glasses. Gluck gave a concert on his own, refined version which used only pure spring water. And Benjamin Franklin followed suit with a 120 glass Armonica on which he played new compositions provided for the occasion by Beethoven and Mozart.

Shortly after this uncharacteristic success, Pockrich returned to form by marrying a woman who, after eight years of running up dressmakers' bills, left him for another man. But Pockrich soldiered on, standing unsuccessfully for the Irish Parliament, and laying plans for the disposition of his body after death. He directed his executors to preserve his corpse in spirits for the benefit of the public, who were to be allowed to gaze upon the remains of this remarkable person. Unfortunately, Pockrich died in a fire in a London coffeehouse so that his last scheme, like so many of its predecessors, came to nothing.

Porson
Richard

Richard Porson, the son of humble parents, was a brilliant classics scholar who was put through Eton and Cambridge by wealthy patrons who recognised his abilities. At Eton, so he said, he learnt nothing; his only pleasant memories of the place were of rat-hunting in the Long Hall.

Porson was fond of novels (an unlikely passion for an eighteenth-century Regius Professor of Greek). He knew the whole of Smollett's *Roderick Random* by heart and often quoted entire chapters at what he deemed appropriate moments. He also had a weakness for Swift's *Tale of a Tub*: and bought every copy of it he came across. He was equally at home with more esoteric works. To a friend who asked him the meaning of a certain word in Thucydides Porson repeated the entire passage in which the word was used. Asked how he knew the particular passage, Porson explained, 'that word occurs only two times in Thucydides, once on the right hand page in the edition which you are using, and once on the left. I observed on which side you looked and accordingly knew to which passage you referred.'

Like Dr Johnson, Porson was an insomniac and preferred to

spend not only his evenings, but also his nights, in the company of a congenial – and often sleepy – group of friends. His capacity to stay up all night caused difficulties in some of the households he frequented until an informal agreement was reached that he be allowed to stay until 11 p.m. provided he left without protest at that time.

This rule only applied to houses where he was a regular visitor. New acquaintances found him harder to eject. After dining with an archbishop and talking until one in the morning, Porson and a friend took their leave. As they walked away, Porson remarked in a miserable voice, 'I hate being turned out-of-doors like a dog.'

John Horne Tooke, knowing of Porson's habits, was careful to ask him to dine on an evening following three successive nights of no sleep. To his dismay, Porson showed no signs of flagging and Tooke was forced to stay up all night talking and drinking with his guest. Breakfast time came and went and Porson was still talking. In desperation Tooke excused himself with an invented story of having to meet someone at a coffee-house in Leicester Square. Porson, all agreeableness and enthusiasm, offered to accompany him and they set forth. Once in the coffee-house, Tooke managed to shake off his guest. He dashed straight home, barred the door and instructed his servant not to admit Porson. 'For,' as he said later, 'a man who could sit up four nights, successively, could sit up forty.'

Porson drank a great deal. Indeed at a time when the standard was for cultivated men literally to drink themselves under the table every night, Porson distinguished himself by his willingness to consume alcohol of any description. Once while dining with John Hoppner, Porson was informed that there would be no wine since Mrs Hoppner, who was out of the house, carried the keys to the wine cellar. Porson, insisting that Mrs Hoppner kept a bottle of gin hidden for her own use, somehow prevailed upon her protesting husband to search her bedroom where, to Mr Hoppner's shock, they did indeed find a bottle. Porson drank it at once and, his thirst quenched, pronounced it most excellent gin. When Mrs Hoppner returned she was confronted by a reproachful husband, an empty bottle and the story of how her perfidy had been discovered. She stood for a minute, taking it in and then said, 'Drunk it! Good God! It was for the lamp.'

Porson's reputation as a learned academic survived his drinking bouts and stories of his 'high animal spirits', exemplified by the tale of his carrying a young lady around the room in his teeth on a wager. There are a host of stories about Porson of the absent-minded professor variety. He sometimes remained incommunicado for days or weeks, absorbed in a passage of his favourite author, Euripides. He was totally unfit for business of any kind, hated travelling, never answered a letter, and once replied, when asked by the poet Rogers to dine, 'Thank you, I dined yesterday.'

He was tall and handsome, but took so little trouble over his appearance as to shock some of his colleagues. A contemporary account describes him 'with a large patch of coarse brown paper on his nose, his rusty black coat hung with cobwebs'. He was often refused admission to his friends' houses by their servants and was once turned away from a restaurant where he had been invited to dine by an acquaintance.

None the less, Porson married in 1796. The wedding took place in the morning, and the bride and groom went off in different directions immediately after. He spent the day with a friend, making no mention of the morning's events. In the evening he dined out and afterwards went to his club as usual. Mrs Porson's reaction is not known, but the union, blissful or not, was brief since she died within a year, without, it seems, making much of a dent in her husband's bachelor habits.

Pottesman
Solomon

A friend once saw Solomon Pottesman coming out of a cinema at which was being shown the Jeanette McDonald-Nelson Eddy musical, *Blossom Time*. Six days later, passing the cinema at the same hour, he again saw Potty emerging. 'So,' he said, 'you've seen the film twice.' 'No, I've been every night,' Potty replied.

The warm theatre was no doubt more appealing than Pottesman's squalid flat near the British Museum. Overflowing with books, it was filthy and furnished with only one creaky old bed. Potty lived alone and never invited friends to his room – indeed he did his best to keep his address a secret. One acquaintance who managed to enter the citadel was embarrassed to realise that he had been given the only cup in the flat while Potty drank his tea from a milk bottle.

The meanness of his surroundings was partly a matter of choice. Apart from a brief period working in a factory during the war Potty had never been employed. He lived by buying and selling antiquarian books. Nothing printed after 1700 interested him; he was primarily a collector of incunabula, or 'inkies', as he called them. Potty sold only as much as necessary to stay alive; he preferred to hoard his treasures. Most of his finds, wrapped in brown paper, were stored in bank vaults or safe-deposit boxes around London. He had a private strongroom beneath Harrods. During the flood season Potty lived in a state of perpetual anxiety that his precious books would be covered by water, yet he stoutly refused to move to higher ground; such a move would have meant leaving the neighbourhood of his beloved British Museum. Instead he disconnected his lavatory cistern so that it could not burst and flood the room. All flushing had to be done with a bucket of water.

His appearance changed little over the years. Indoors or out he wore a cloth cap. The same brown shirt appeared every day, with two or three copies of *The Times* wrapped around him as an underlayer in cold weather. His ties were made to last by the device of tying the knot so as to obscure any stains, until at last the wide part of the tie was directly under his chin and the narrow back layer hung well past his waist.

In many ways Potty was an exasperation to his colleagues. Living alone, he kept his own time, and didn't understand why his friends could not drop everything when he came by for a few hours of chit-chat during business hours. According to Alan Thomas, a fellow bookseller, there were only two occasions on which Potty was forced to be aware of 'outside' time: the opening of an auction and the closing of the Reading Room at the British Museum.

His behaviour at auctions was atrocious. In spite of a lifetime spent in auction rooms, Potty never quite mastered the art of bidding; often he got excited and bid against himself. He distracted fellow buyers who were trying to bid by talking about his latest purchase. He walked about the room obscuring other bidders. When the time came to collect his books, Potty took at least a quarter of an hour to write out a single cheque: even then he was reluctant to part with it. He kept taking it back to examine it, explaining in a plaintive voice, 'I once made a mistake in writing a cheque.'

Finally he would unfold the greasy brown paper he carried

everywhere and laboriously wrap his purchases. Never was he seen without a number of brown paper parcels done up with string. When in recent years the British Museum introduced security checks, it was bad luck indeed to be behind Potty at the guard's desk as he agonisingly slowly untied and then rewrapped his packages for the inspectors.

In spite of his odd behaviour, Potty was regarded with respect and affection by his colleagues. He had a place of honour at Sothebys – the only outsider permitted to sit at the staff table. His knowledge of incunabula, though he was an entirely self-taught bibliophile, was equalled only by a few scholars. He made several important discoveries, including evidence of the existence of a new Shakespeare play. Potty knew the contents of the British Museum Library better than almost anyone else – not only the names, but the shelf numbers of many of the books.

Potty died in 1978, after a protracted illness. While in hospital it cheered him to tell friends the name of the book in which the disease which was to kill him had first been mentioned, and to recall with a contented smile, 'I've *had* that book.'

Robertson
James

obertson, who was born in Perthshire, was a devoted supporter of the Jacobite cause. He fought in the 1745 rebellion and was briefly imprisoned in Edinburgh, but the authorities decided he was harmless and released him. While in prison he earned his nickname, 'The Daft Highland Laird' because of his cheerful acceptance of incarceration. He was much cast down by being ejected from prison because he wanted above all else to be a martyr to the Stuart cause. As one writer put it, 'in his anxiety to be hanged, drawn and quartered as a rebel partisan', Robertson did everything he could to incite arrest. He drank the Pretender's health in public and spoke treason in the streets, but the authorities turned a blind eye.

Finally, Robertson was forced, in order to get back into prison, to resort to common crime. He was arrested for refusing to pay his rent. Friends paid his debt, but Robertson stoutly refused to vacate his cell unless brought to trial for high treason. One morning two soldiers presented themselves and announced that they had been sent to escort the Laird to court where judges were assembled to try him for treason. He gladly preceded them out of his cell, but the instant he stepped into the street the soldiers jumped back into the building and locked him out.

After this disappointment Robertson lost heart and turned his mind to other matters. Chiefly, he made wooden figures of his heroes and enemies which he mounted on staffs and displayed on his walks about Edinburgh. He became a popular figure, well known for his habit of handing out snuff and tobacco to adults and his own home-made toys to the children he met.

Robinson
Matthew

Mr Robinson, as he was until he inherited his uncle's title in 1793 at the age of eighty-one, was a singularly high-principled person. He resigned after two terms as Member of Parliament because of his disgust with the corruption of party politics. He himself voted independently. As a result he had enemies in both parties, though he was popular with the people. To his sister, the bluestocking, Mrs Montagu, who reproached him for some social solecism shortly after his elevation to the peerage, he shrugged, 'You know I was born a democrat.'

Robinson had strong views on the subjects of fresh air and exercise. He walked everywhere, although he often took a carriage along for his servants, who had less stamina than he did and, as he remarked, finer clothes that were worth protecting from bad weather. At home the windows were perpetually open and he seldom lit a fire. He spurned alcohol and believed that the English countryside produced sufficient to support the English people and that it was wicked to eat 'exotics' such as wheat. Robinson's diet consisted mainly of beef tea, but, because of his democratic beliefs, guests at his table could order whatever they liked.

Robinson was a good and popular landlord. He never raised rents and he practised a peculiar system of land management, based on his political and philosophical principles, at Mount Morris, his 800-acre estate in east Kent. There were no fences, gates or stiles; trees were never felled, nothing was planted, and the gardens were returned to nature. But Robinson knew a great deal about grazing, so the black sheep and cattle that roamed freely on his land did well.

Robinson's appearance was striking, largely due to his simple dress and a beard which, by the end of his life, reached to his knees. His moustache was long enough for him to be able to tuck the ends behind his ears. Country people often took him for a Turk and his friends felt, rather sadly, that his strange looks and odd manners detracted from the seriousness of his philosophy.

He had several pet hates, notably doctors and the Bank of England. The latter he believed was certain sooner or later to fail. He made a £10 bet to that effect with a Canterbury alderman and bound his heirs to continue the wager after his death. Robinson was a great believer in the beneficial effects of water. He installed drinking fountains all along the roads of his property and always stopped to give a few coins to anyone he saw drinking from them. Every morning he bathed his eyes in salt water and that was just the beginning of his regimen. Robinson spent hours on end completely immersed in water, often until he fainted. He had a special bathing house built at Mount Morris with a glass front and a thatched roof. Here, sitting up to his neck in his favourite liquid, he ate his meals, received visitors, worked on his political pamphlets, and planned the management of the estate.

Robinson's sister told of how she learned of a trip her brother had made to a fashionable watering-place. She was taking a tour of the resort when her guide pointed out where Mr Robinson had bathed with a roast loin of veal floating at his side. 'The Quality', Mrs Montagu reported her guide as saying, 'did make a great Wonderment at it, but it was nice veal and he gave what he did not eat of it to her and some others; to be sure he was the particularest gentleman she had ever heard of, but he was very good-natured.'

Ros
Amanda McKettrick

Amanda Ros of Larne, Co. Antrim, the author of *Irene Iddlesleigh* and *Delina Delaney*, had printed on her cards: 'At Home Always To The Honourable'. To her the dishonourable were a large and powerful group, the least desirable element of which was the critics, or as she called them 'donkeyosities', 'egotistical earthworms', 'evil-minded snapshots of spleen', 'poisonous apes', and 'talent wipers of wormy order'.

The first such 'clay crab of corruption' to arouse Mrs Ros's wrath was Barry Pain, who in 1898 reviewed *Irene Iddlesleigh*, calling it 'The Book of The Century'. Pain's review opens with a long-winded and confusing sentence; it goes on to say: 'That is a long and rocky sentence, but if you go slowly at it and worry it, you will find that it has a meaning. That is one of the principal respects in which it differs from *Irene Iddlesleigh* by Mrs

145

Amanda McKettrick Ros.' Through no fault of the author's, he said, *Irene Iddlesleigh* was one of the funniest books he had ever read. This did not soothe Mrs Ros's ruffled feelings and her next novel carried a preface attacking 'this so-called Barry Pain'.

This served well as a warning to other 'hogwashing hooligans' and Wyndham Lewis showed his apprehension in reviewing the second edition thirty years later: 'One has to be careful about this fine book', he wrote. 'I am going to be extremely careful about this superb book.' Not careful enough, it seems, for soon Mrs Ros had dubbed him St Scandalbags.

Her literary style was highly individual. Besides her flair for abusive nicknames, she took alliteration as a tool of dramatic narrative to new heights. An excerpt from Irene Iddlesleigh's soliloquy on her wedding night will give an idea: 'Leave me now deceptive demons of deluded mockery; lurk no more around the vale of vanity, like a vindictive viper, strike the lyre of living deception to the strains of dull deadness, despair and doubt . . . .'

Her talent for naming puts Mrs Ros, in her own way, on a par with Dickens. In her unpublished novel, 'Helen Huddleston', she gives free rein to her creative impulses while at the same time demonstrating a finely tuned awareness of social distinctions. Members of the aristocracy, Lord Raspberry and his sister Cherry, Sir Peter Plum, the Earl of Grape, and Sir Christopher Currant, are all named after fruits, while the maid, Lily Lentil, takes her surname from a common vegetable.

Amanda Ros had a small but perceptive band of followers who, far from being put off by the criticism her books received were encouraged by it to delve still further into her work and who formed clubs to discuss their favourite author. Until the 1930s when her books were reprinted by Chatto & Windus, copies were difficult to obtain because Mrs Ros, distrusting publishers, always printed and published her own writings. Members of the Oxford Amanda Ros Society (established in 1907 to hold weekly readings of Ros) often copied out sections in longhand to pass around to friends and family.

This was, naturally, gratifying, but Amanda Ros needed no one to remind her that she was a genius. She took her gift very seriously, always signed herself 'Amanda Ros, Author', and accepted as her due the palms offered by those she referred to as 'the million and one who thirst for aught that drops from my pen'. To one fan she wrote, apropos of a projected new work, 'I hope that when you have the pleasure of digesting its pages that you will add to its long list of expected admirers.' She toyed with the idea of applying for the Nobel Prize in 1930, when she discovered it was worth £9,000 but decided against it on the grounds that the judges, like all members of the literary establishment, were probably too corrupt to award it to an outsider.

For the last forty years of her life, Amanda wrote only poetry. She remains best known for her prose works, but one verse may suffice to show that she had poetic talents which are not unworthy of the great McGonagall.

'On Visiting Westminster Abbey'

Holy Moses! Take a look!
Flesh decayed in every nook,
Some rare bits of brain lie here,
Mortal loads of beef and beer.

Sackville-West
Victoria-Josefa

panish passion and Anglo-Saxon reserve were united in Lady Sackville – the illegitimate child of a Latin dancer and an English diplomat – to create a contradictory and unpredictable temperament. Her attitude towards money, for example, veered without warning from reckless indulgence to extreme parsimony. In certain moods money slipped through her hands like water: she once absentmindedly left a £10,000 cheque from J P Morgan made out to bearer in a taxi; on another occasion a stranger whom she met on the forty-minute train journey from London to Sevenoaks and never again laid eyes on persuaded her to invest £60,000 in a gold mine. In neither case was the money recovered.

On the other hand for a time she took to cutting up used postage stamps and piecing together the non-postmarked bits to save the cost of a new stamp. She also economised by writing letters on filched hotel notepaper, the backs of advertisements, and on one occasion on a slice of cooked ham. She was especially pleased with toilet paper pinched from Harrod's ladies room. She corresponded regularly on this for quite some time and praised it to her daughter, the writer Vita Sackville-West, for taking ink so nicely.

Lady Sackville was a high-spirited woman, capable of being utterly charming, but with a quick, if short-lived, temper. Those closest to her, her servants and her family, suffered the brunt of her mood changes, though they did not always take it lying down: several times the entire household staff resigned *en masse*. One much loved nanny was summarily dismissed on suspicion of having eaten three-dozen quail which had not arrived in time for a dinner party.

Fresh air was one of Lady Sackville's great passions. She never had a fire in her room, kept the windows and doors at Knole always open, and insisted upon taking her meals outdoors in all weathers. Often a meal with her meant sitting wrapped in fur coats with a hot water bottle on one's knees and a rug draped over one's lap. A lamp provided some light in the darkness and illuminated the drifting snowflakes as they piled up on the food and the cutlery. The compensation for all this was Lady Sackville saying cosily, 'Now, aren't you deliciously warm?' Luckily, she was apparently immune to colds; her favourite remedy for sore throats was to tie a pair of the architect Edwin Lutyens's old socks around her neck.

Knole, the ancient Sackville home in the Kentish countryside, was Lady Sackville's pride and joy. There and at various smaller houses that she bought and sold over the years, she was able to put her peculiar notions of interior decoration into practice. One bedroom at Knole was papered entirely with postage stamps. The risers of a staircase at another house were painted to look like bookshelves. The Persian Room was furnished completely with objects from Turkey, a geographical contradiction which Lady Sackville absolutely refused to acknowledge. She took great trouble over minor details, and had a special individually designed bookplate printed for each book she owned.

Her daughter Vita was of course a distinguished gardener, as well as a writer, but Lady Sackville preferred artificial flowers. Tin delphiniums were among her favourites because, as she explained to Vita, they are always in bloom and never plagued by slugs. Rather than planting living things, she often landscaped using only potted plants and porcelain flowers. On one occasion when Vita was coming to lunch, Lady Sackville's garden looked particularly dismal and, wanting to make a show for her daughter, she sent a friend out to buy £30 worth of velvet, sequined, paper, beaded and satin flowers which she 'planted' in an artistic arrangement in the bare earth.

An expensive lawsuit about the Sackville title had eaten into the family's fortune and Lady Sackville worried constantly that Knole's upkeep would become too expensive for them. When Lionel, her husband, was called up for the First World War, she wrote directly to Lord Kitchener saying that he must not be posted to a dangerous position as Knole could not possibly survive the massive death duties that would fall due if he was killed.

Later she wrote to complain that Knole was being deprived of its staff by the call-up: 'I think perhaps you do not realize, my dear Lord K., that we employ five carpenters and four painters and two blacksmiths and two footmen and you are taking them all from us! I do not complain about the footmen, although I must say that I had never thought I would see parlourmaids at Knole!. . . . Dear Lord K., I am sure you will sympathize with me when I say that parlourmaids are so middle-class, not at all what you and me are used to. But, as I said, that is not what I complain about. . . . I know that we must give an example. You are at the War Office and must neglect your dear Broome, which you love so much. I think you love it as much as I love Knole? and of course you must love it even more because the world says you have never loved any woman – is that true? I shall ask you next time I come to luncheon with you. But talking about luncheon reminds me of parlourmaids, and I said that I would not complain about them (because I am patriotic after all) but I do complain about the way you take our workmen from us.'

The distinction between charitable enterprises and profit-making ones eluded Lady Sackville. She was not in the least shy of soliciting funds on her own behalf – sometimes without actually saying so. The energy, invention and ruthless charm she put into such enterprises was staggering. One of her pet 'charities' in later years was The Homeless Sleeping on Brighton Beach, an organisation which was not registered with the Charity Commissioners and of which she was the only known member or beneficiary.

In 1928 she wrote letters to all her acquaintances asking for donations to her Roof of Friendship Fund. Each person was asked to give the price of a tile to be dedicated to his or her friendship with Lady Sackville and to form with all the others an inspirational symbol of friendship to replace her distinctly uninspiring and leaky roof. Quite a few did contribute, but she was furious with William Nicholson, who had the effrontery to send in a real tile.

Later on came the Million Penny Fund, designed to eliminate the National Debt. Lady Sackville perused the papers for mentions of famous people celebrating their birthdays and wrote asking them to contribute one penny for each year of their life. The form letter she had written for the purpose ended with a plea: 'and do give me three stamped envelopes which means one for my begging letter, one for having the pleasure of thanking you, and one for a fresh VICTIM.'

Another time she decided to hold a white elephant sale. 'You know, people have them at bazaars,' she told Vita, 'but I shall have this one for myself. And then I thought as elephants come from Siam I would write to the King and ask him for a white one.' To the surprise of everyone but Lady Sackville, the King of Siam replied with a gift of a small but valuable solid-silver elephant.

Seymour
Charles

The Duke of Somerset had the good fortune in 1682 to marry Elizabeth Percy, heir to the ancient titles and immense wealth of the Earldom of Northumberland. The acquisition of her riches and prestige turned Somerset from a merely proud man to an extraordinary model of self-conceit.

Although he loved pomp and eagerly participated in ceremonial occasions, where he cut a handsome figure, Somerset's sensibility was offended by the notion of the lower orders witnessing his magnificent person on these or any other occasions and he took elaborate steps to prevent such a distressing occurrence. He built houses at intervals along the main roads between London and his estates so that he would not be obliged to suffer the indignity of staying at a common inn. Outriders preceded him to clear the road of commoners, whom they unceremoniously ordered out of the way. Somerset was just as reluctant to see such people as he was to be seen by them. He had to communicate with his servants, of course, but rather than speak to them he used sign language. Not surprisingly he became known as 'The Proud Duke'.

Somerset's family was not exempt from the effects of his pride. His youngest daughter, Charlotte, used to sit and watch her father as he took his after-dinner nap on a couch. One day she wandered away while he slept and he rolled onto the floor. He woke in a fury and ordered the whole household to ostracise her. Everyone was too intimidated to mention Charlotte's name to the Duke, even to ask when they were to be allowed to speak to her, so for a year she was completely ostracised. Later she was deprived of £20,000 of her inheritance for sitting down in his presence.

When Somerset's second wife, herself the daughter of the Earl of Nottingham, tapped him gently with her fan, he said to her icily, 'Madame, my *first* Duchess was a Percy and *she* never took such a liberty.'

Sitwell
Sir George Reresby

Although Sir George Sitwell lived in the nineteenth and twentieth centuries, his heart and mind were in the fourteenth. He was lord of the manor of Eckington in Derbyshire for eighty-one years, a position that suited him to perfection, or would have if the world hadn't changed so much in the past 500 years. A sign in his house ran: 'I must ask anyone entering the house never to contradict me in any way, as it interferes with the functioning of the gastric juices and prevents my sleeping at night.'

His interests, though obscure, were wide-ranging. Seven sitting-rooms at Renishaw Hall were co-opted to serve as his studies. All were littered with books and notes, each subject filed in its own specially constructed box. Some of the more intriguing titles for possible future monographs were:

The Black Death at Rotherham
The Use of the Bed
Osbert's Debts
Acorns as an Article of Medieval Diet
Sachie's Mistakes
Pig Keeping in the Thirteenth Century
The History of the Fork
Domestic Manners in Sheffield in the Year 1250
My Advice on Poetry
Lepers' Squints
Wool-Gathering in Medieval Times and Since
The Errors of Modern Parents
The Eckington Dump
The Origin of the Word Gentleman
The History of the Cold
My Inventions

Any article on the last subject would have to include the Sitwell Egg. With a yolk of smoked meat, a white of compressed rice and a shell of synthetic lime, this was intended to be a convenient and nourishing meal for travellers. Sir George decided to put the marketing of his egg into the experienced hands of Mr Gordon Selfridge, founder of the famous Oxford Street shop.

Wearing a silk hat and frock coat, he appeared in Selfridge's office one morning without an appointment, and announced, 'I'm Sir George Sitwell and I've brought my egg with me.' He told no one what Selfridge said, but soon after this encounter the egg project was quietly shelved. There were other inventions, however, including a musical toothbrush that played 'Annie Laurie' and a small revolver for killing wasps.

Sir George's strength of personality was matched by that of his three talented children, or nearly so, for although they all managed successful careers of their own in the end, his disapproval of virtually everything they did was a major factor in their development. When Osbert announced that he was thinking of writing a novel, he was told, 'Oh I shouldn't do that if I were you! You'd better drop the idea at once. My cousin, Stephen Arthington, had a friend who utterly ruined his health writing a novel!' Of Edith's literary aspirations, his comment was: 'Edith made a great mistake by not going in for lawn tennis.' He was also an enthusiastic advocate of gymnastics: 'Nothing a young man likes so much as a girl who's good at the parallel bars.' This is at least as useful a piece of advice as another of his favourite maxims: 'Nothing makes a man so popular as singing after dinner.' Sitwell's attitude towards his children is summarised in his comment to Osbert: 'It is dangerous for you to lose touch with me for a single day. You never know when you may need the benefit of my experience and advice.'

Losing touch for as many days as possible became a major preoccupation for Osbert and Sacheverell who invented a mythical yacht, the Rover, and had headed notepaper printed on which they wrote to their father regretting that as the itinerary was as yet unsettled they could not give him an address where they might be contacted. All this time they were in London or Italy, but in spite of Sir George's not infrequent excursions to both places, they were in little danger of being discovered since he rarely recognised his children outside the home.

Of course the temptation, one might almost say the need, to tease such a father was great. Sir George was particularly vulnerable with regard to modern developments, say since 1650. He knew nothing of modern slang. Shocked by the bad behaviour of an acquaintance who had offered him a piece of jewelry and failed to deliver it, Sir George complained to Osbert about modern manners, 'Such a pity to promise people things and then forget about them. It is most inconsiderate – really inexcusable.' The cause of this lament was the parting remark: 'I'll give you a ring, Sir George, on Thursday.'

At one period Osbert used the word 'blotto' frequently and deliberately until his father finally rose to the bait and asked what it meant. He seemed interested to learn that it was slang for very tired. Shortly afterwards he took the opportunity of demonstrating how *au fait* he was with modern ways by suggesting to two guests that they take a rest after lunch as they both seemed quite blotto. The children once got him to book a month's holiday at a lunatic asylum by representing it as a charming retreat, affectionately nicknamed 'the bin' by a core of loyal residents who could hardly bear to tear themselves away.

Sir George's ignorance of, or refusal to acknowledge, the facts of modern life was extraordinary. He proposed, in the 1930s, an artists' ball, to which he suggested inviting Degas, Renoir, Rodin and Sergeant. For a while farming was his passion and he gave his long-suffering agent many valuable hints on how it was done in the fourteenth century. During this time he tried to pay, whenever possible, in kind: offering pigs and potatoes to Eton for Sacheverell's school fees. Osbert managed to get his allowance paid in currency, but his father arrived at the proper amount by studying the allowance granted the eldest son of the Lord of the Eckington Manor at the time of the Black Death. Lady Ida, Sir George's wife, got involved with an unscrupulous money-lender and, when her husband refused on principle to bail her out, became the centre of a painful and notorious lawsuit. This dreadful experience confirmed Sir George in his misanthropic views – as he said to Osbert, '*Such* a mistake to have friends.' – and drove him even further into the life of a recluse.

Sir George was acutely conscious of his many acts of generosity. What some misguided people saw as meddling, was, as he knew only too well, self-sacrifice: the dedication of his time and thought to advance the good of others. This could be wearying and occasionally he gave vent to an exhausted plea for understanding. To a Salvation Army lass soliciting funds for Self-Denial Week, he sighed, 'For *some* people, self-denial week is *every* week.'

He gave Osbert the benefit of his experience when in 1914 he wrote from Scarborough to his son, who was then an officer in the trenches: 'though you will not, of course, have to encounter anywhere abroad the same weight of gunfire that your mother and I had to face here, yet my experience may be useful to you. Directly you hear the first shell retire, as I did, to the Undercroft, and remain there quietly until all firing has ceased. Even then a bombardment . . . is a strain upon the nervous system – but the best remedy for that, as always, is to keep warm and have plenty of plain, nourishing food at frequent but regular intervals. And, of course, plenty of rest, I find a nap in the afternoon most helpful . . . and I advise you to try it whenever possible.'

Among his characteristic acts were banning electricity from Renishaw during his lifetime; limiting guests to two candles apiece; and insisting that the family drink cold boiled water rather than wine during travels in Italy.

On his journeys alone through Italy Sir George stayed at very primitive inns, quite often sharing a dormitory with eight or ten other men in what was little more than a doss house. But he had with him his valet, Henry Moat, known as 'the Great Man', whose responsibility it was to rig the mosquito net each night and lay out the formal evening dress in which Sir George insisted on appearing for dinner at these tumbledown inns. The mosquito net was basic equipment – at home and abroad – for someone with Sir George's dread of disease and germs. He travelled with an extensive supply of medicines, all mislabelled to discourage – or at least to punish – anybody wanting to sample. His inflatable air cushion, another ever-present companion, was doughnut-shaped so that Sir George could slip it over his arm when not using it.

Decorating his two houses, Renishaw in Derbyshire and Montegufoni in Italy, and redesigning their gardens were Sir George's major passions. He spent enormous sums of money and a great deal of his own and other people's time on an endless succession of alterations and improvements. As Henry Moat said, 'He never entered any place, but he commenced pulling down and building up.'

Sir George thought nothing of lowering lawns by several feet, making hills, relocating vast trees, creating or draining lakes. He had schemes for constructing or importing fountains, aqueducts, cascades, and statues of all descriptions. Four thousand men were set to work on an artificial lake at Renishaw. A plan was mooted to stencil Chinese blue-willow patterns on his white cows, but the cows' objections put an end to the project. Wooden survey towers loomed out of the lake to provide a vantage point for plotting further changes in the landscape.

156

Nothing was ever completed, but that didn't prevent new projects being planned. And each new scheme struck terror into someone's heart: visiting his son Sacheverell's home at Weston in Northamptonshire in 1924, Sir George casually remarked as he looked out across the grounds, 'I don't propose to do much here; just a sheet of water and a line of statues.'

2nd Earl of Masserene
Skeffington
Clotworthy

For the first fifteen years of his life – until he inherited his father's title and became the 2nd Earl of Masserene – Clotworthy Skeffington had – in his name – a cruel burden to bear. Perhaps this explains his subsequent odd behaviour.

In 1770 on a visit to Paris, Masserene became involved in a business venture which he did not understand, but which none the less resulted in his being imprisoned for debt. Rather than tacitly admit his guilt by paying up, Masserene resolved to stay in jail for twenty-five years, after which time, according to French law, his debts would be cancelled. His incarceration was made more bearable than most, by the expenditure of £4,000 a year. Friends and mistresses were only too eager to pay visits to the comfortably appointed cell in which Masserene's private chef produced lavish dinners.

While in jail he married Marie Anne Barcier, the beautiful daughter of the prison governor. She made two unsuccessful attempts to help him escape. Finally, in 1789, after eighteen years in prison, Lord Messerene was released from La Force the day before the storming of the Bastille, by a mob whose enthusiasm for opening the gate was at least partly fuelled by bribes from Lady Masserene.

Once freed, he returned to Antrim Castle, his seat in Ireland, and took an active part in the battle against Jacobism. Masserene formed his own yeomanry to defend against an anticipated Jacobite uprising, and trained it in his own peculiar fashion. The men were drilled without weapons; they simulated rifle shots by clapping their hands and presented arms in a complicated pantomime involving a series of hand signals. He also developed a number of new drills with names such as Serpentine and Eel-in-the-Mud. All this military activity convinced Masserene that he was a natural leader of men, a phenomenon unappreciated by the military establishment of the time.

Masserene continued to indulge his personal whims. From time to time he ordered the dining table, completely set, all the chairs and an elaborate dinner, to be put on the roof. What could not be carried by hand was hoisted through the window on pulleys. Once the party was seated at the relocated table and about to start their alfresco meal, Masserene usually declared himself dissatisfied and ordered everything back inside. When his wife's dog died, all the local dogs were invited – some would say ordered – to its funeral at Antrim Castle. Fifty of them, provided with white scarves, acted as a guard of honour.

In 1800, Masserene's loyal French wife, whom he had never fully appreciated, died. Shortly thereafter he married a servant girl, who, with her family and her lover, succeeded in gaining control of Masserene's fortune, before he died in 1805.

Spence
Thomas

Thomas Spence advocated a number of changes in Britain's political system and way of life. Among his ideas was a scheme to increase the working man's leisure time by switching from a seven- to a five-day week, thus increasing by twenty-one the number of Sundays in one year. He also developed a phonetic spelling system for English. Initially, of course, the new method might pose problems for those used to the old-fashioned way of writing English, but Spence's way was based on logic and, as he pointed out, 'it shud be eze inuf too no it bi a litil aplikashin and praktis.'

Spence came to London from Newcastle and set up a stall in Holborn where he published pamphlets and sold a gruel made of crushed orchid roots. One of his publications was a rhyming version of Tom Paine's, *The Rights of Man* in 1783. His advocacy of land nationalisation brought Spence into disrepute with the authorities, who repeatedly arrested him for seditious libel, though he was convicted only once.

Spence had an ingenious method of publicising his ideas: leaning out of a window, he tossed copper medallions struck with appropriate images and slogans at passers-by. One medal, with a picture of a cat, warned that 'he could be stroked down, but would not suffer himself to be rubbed against the grain'; another announced that Spence's plan for a better world would bring about 'in fact, the Millennium'.

Although he was known as an honest and warm-hearted man, Spence's private life was not successful. He had an unhappy first marriage. His second wife was a housemaid whom he met when she answered the door at a house where he had business; they were married later the same day and soon after she ran away with another man.

His political ideas, however, brought him many admirers; his disciples, calling themselves Spenceans, carried on his work after his death in 1814.

Spencer
Herbert

Spencer was an immensely influential social philosopher who proclaimed the rights of the individual over the state, and an early defender of the theory of organic evolution. The phrase 'survival of the fittest' is his, and Darwin called Spencer 'twenty times my superior'. His monumental works of philosophy were written at a great cost to his health. As a result he learned to cosset himself. When he went for a drive he periodically signalled to the coachman to pull up, regardless of traffic, while he took his pulse to determine whether or not the journey should continue.

At home Spencer needed quiet. If the ladies with whom he lodged tried to engage him in conversation at a bad time he replied with a terse, 'Mustn't talk now' and inserted his specially designed velvet ear plugs. Usually he dined with his landladies, but if circumstances were unfavourable to a good digestion – if, for example, he was to be seated opposite a person he considered unattractive, or if the conversation promised to be too stimulating – he preferred to eat alone in his rooms. On days at home Spencer wore his woolly bear suit. This one-piece garment, designed by the great philosopher himself, eliminated the need for separate boots, trousers, shirt and coat, and was extremely comfortable, though it did make him look like a large brown grizzly.

For Spencer, and those who looked after him, setting out on even a short excursion was no easy task. His travelling equipment – a carrying chair, a hammock, various rugs and air cushions, as well as his luggage and his current manuscript done up in brown paper and secured to him by a thick cord tied around his waist – required at least two attendants. One of their chief jobs was to hang Spencer's hammock in his train compartment at the start of the journey. Spencer always climbed in at once, preferring the hammock's gentle swaying to the harsh jarring of the ordinary seats.

But Spencer also had a mischievous sense of humour. In his younger days as a civil engineer he played a prolonged practical joke on one of his colleagues. He began by placing a strip of paper inside the man's hatband, adding another strip every day for a period of weeks so that the poor man became convinced that his head was growing at an alarming rate – the more so after Spencer had treated him to a lurid description of the symptoms of water on the brain.

4th Earl of Harrington
Lord Petersham
Stanhope
Charles

One of the great Regency dandies and an intimate of the Prince Regent, Petersham was in a position and of a disposition to set fashion rather than follow it. He had a passion for brown, inspired, it is thought, by his love for a charming widow of that name; his entire equipage – horses, carriage inside and out, and liveries for driver and out-riders – was of that colour.

He lent his name to the Petersham greatcoat and the Harrington hat, which, with its tapering crown and square brim turned up at the sides, enjoyed a brief vogue before passing into well-deserved obscurity. When he was a neophyte in the world of fashion, Petersham took the trouble to cut out all his own clothes to ensure a proper fit. He also made his boot blacking to a secret recipe believed to contain champagne. As he grew older he dressed to accentuate what he thought was a strong resemblance to Henry IV.

Petersham never went out of his house before six in the evening. His days were occupied with his collections of teas, snuffs, and snuff boxes, of which he was a connoisseur. Captain Gronow, that marvellous Regency gossip, described Petersham's sitting room as 'more like a shop than a gentleman's sitting room. All around the walls were shelves, upon which were placed the cannisters containing congou, pekoe, souchong, bohea, gunpowder, Russian, and many other teas, all the best of their kind; on the other side of the room were beautiful jars; with names in gilt letters, of innumerable kinds of snuff, and all the necessary apparatus for moistening and mixing.' Petersham had a snuff box for every day of the year and firm ideas about how they ought to be used. Of one, a light-blue box of S`evres porcelain, he said, 'Yes, it is a nice summer box, but it would not do for winter wear.'

'Walking Stewart'
Stewart
John

After serving as a writer in the East India Company, a general in Hyder Ali's army, and Prime Minister to the Nabob of Arcot, John Stewart, thirty-four years of age, decided to return to England. He walked all the way, passing through India, Persia, Ethiopia, Arabia, Turkey, and Lapland. When he arrived home, Stewart spoke eight languages besides English. His pedestrian feats did not cease at this point. Stewart subsequently made walking tours of Europe and the New World and once walked from London up to Scotland just to have a chat with Dugold Stewart.

Once in London he made a name for himself by frequenting public places in Armenian national costume and handing out leaflets in which he set forth his philosophical opinions. Stewart was a great advocate of fresh air and exercise. Every morning he sat among the cows in St James Park and inhaled their breath, which he maintained had a therapeutic effect on him. In the middle of one of his books on metaphysics, Stewart devotes a page to the dangers of damp beds and sheets. He always carried enough poison to enable him to commit suicide – a relic perhaps of his days in the East – though he died of natural causes in 1822 at the age of seventy-three.

He was an atheist and a sometime vegetarian, but the cornerstone of Stewart's philosophy was his doctrine of the transmutation of atoms. The gist of this is that atoms from the surface of everybody and everything are in constant interchange. 'The human body emits every hour half a pound of matter', Stewart declared. This matter is replaced by that given off by whatever is close at hand – another person, a dog, even, as his disgusted critics suggested, a dunghill. From this Stewart argued that the only logical approach to all people, animals and inanimate objects – of which we are literally a part – was one of respect and compassion.

In 1813 Stewart received £10,000 as compensation in a claim against his former employer, the Nabob of Arcot. Previously near poverty, he was now able to take luxurious apartments in Northumberland Street and begin entertaining. Stewart decorated his new abode by projecting giant magic-lantern slides on the blank walls and covering the rest with mirrors, anticipating the light shows of the 1960s. He also started a series of musical evenings which, remarked a contemporary, 'were rendered less attractive than they might have been by his habit of giving a philosophical lecture previous to the commencement of the music.'

De Quincey admired Stewart, calling him a man of great genius and eloquence, a judgment with which Stewart himself wholeheartedly agreed. De Quincey added, however, that Stewart 'was a man of genius, but not a man of talents, at least his genius was out of all proportion to his talents.' None the less, Stewart was satisfied that 'in the event of my personal dissolution by death, I have communicated all the discoveries my unique mind possesses in the great master-science of men and nature.' He dated his books as if a new era began with their publication; thus 'the first day of Intellectual Life from the era of this work'.

In an attempt to give his ideas the public notice he felt they deserved, Stewart conceived a plan – never executed – of having his name engraved in giant letters on a projecting rock in the Atlantic so that transoceanic voyagers, noticing his name, might be tempted to study his writings.

Stewart's greatest worry was that his wisdom – essential to the happiness of future generations – might be destroyed by tyrants or obscured by the passage of time. As a precaution against the latter he asked De Quincey to translate his works into Latin in case English should fall into desuetude. To protect against the former, readers were urged to bury Stewart's books, properly secured against damp, seven or eight feet underground. The location was to be kept a secret and passed on to a trusted friend as one lay on one's deathbed. In this way Stewart's thoughts would be preserved from the depredations of his enemies and kept alive for a future generation of scholars. De Quincey buried several of Stewart's books. The *Harp of Apollo* (referred to by its author as 'this unparalled work of human energy') is 7 feet under De Quincey's orchard in Grasmere at the bottom of Mount Fairfield.

Strachey
William

William Strachey, one of the great Strachey clan of Indian civil servants and an uncle of Lytton, spent five years in Calcutta as a writer for the East India Company. He returned to England in 1843 and retired from the service in 1848. For the remaining fifty-six years of his life, Strachey lived according to what he considered the only accurate time system in the world, Calcutta time – 5 hours and 54 minutes ahead of Greenwich Mean Time. This meant, of course, that he was quite out of step with the rest of English society. His life, as one nephew said, was like the snark's, who 'frequently breakfasts at five o'clock tea, and dines on the following day'.

As Strachey enjoyed company, this regimen had its drawbacks, but after a number of years he became addicted to it. At one time he thought of trying to change and with this end in mind he bought a mechanical bed that had been displayed at the Paris Exhibition. The bed was connected to an alarm clock and at a pre-set hour each morning the sleepy occupant was thrown onto the floor to face a new day. Strachey's first night in his new bed was terminated by his being ejected neatly into an unfortunately placed full bath. In a fury he smashed the clock and the bed and went back to the only thing he could trust – Calcutta time.

Nevertheless, he managed for many years to keep up a social life, enjoying a reputation as a man about town and working on special assignments for the Colonial Office. He continued to dress in the style of his younger days and always wore galoshes, indoors or out, fair weather or foul.

It was William Strachey who caused the family doctor to comment that no member of the Strachey family would ever go mad. They were, he said, too eccentric for that.

6th Earl of Aldborough
Stratford
Benjamin O'Neale II

The 6th Earl came from an interesting family. His great-grandfather, John Stratford, the 1st Earl of Aldborough (1689–1777), had upon receiving the title styled himself 'the Earl of Aldborough in the Palatine of Upper Ormonde', a place as fictitious as the pedigree he commissioned tracing the family back to William the Conqueror's right-hand man. The new family arms, at least, were quite authentic: they belonged to Alexander the Great.

The 2nd Earl, the extravagant and ostentatious Edward Augustus Stratford had a building mania. He built Aldborough House in Dublin; a seaside home just outside the Irish capital; a model town called Stratford-on-Slaney in County Wicklow; Stratford Place and Stratford House in London, as well as making extensive improvements to Belan, the great house built by his father in County Kildare. His death in 1801 interrupted a strange house party at Belan to which the Earl had invited most of the young people he knew with the intention of marrying them off to one another. He left fifty-four wills.

Edward's brother, John, the 3rd Earl, who died in 1823, had a very sociable wife and daughter, but he hated company. The first, and usually the only, remark guests to his house heard from their host was, 'When do you leave? The coach passes Belan every morning and I can send you there tomorrow.' He rose early to pick the ripe fruit from the garden and hide it from the despised visitors.

Benjamin O'Neill Stratford II, the 6th Earl, distinguished himself by the strength of his devotion to a hot-air balloon. For twenty years he lived only to complete what was going to be the largest balloon in the world – close to 50-feet high when inflated. He shut himself away in Stratford Lodge, 40 miles from Dublin, with only one trustworthy servant; all his meals were cooked in Dublin and sent up daily in the Mail Coach.

The Earl's plan was to fly from Ireland to England and on across the Channel to France, where he had purchased a plot of land on the banks of the Seine as a landing ground. When the Crimean War broke out Lord Aldborough decided to extend his voyage and contribute to the British war effort by flying on across Europe, sniping at Russian officers. Unfortunately for his patriotic dreams, the war came to an end before the balloon was ready. Even more tragically, the balloon hangar caught fire in 1856 and in spite of frantic efforts to save it, the silk balloon was damaged beyond repair.

The Earl lived for a time in the burnt-out hangar but eventually he moved to Alicante, Spain, where he became a recluse in a hotel. He had his meals sent up to him, but refused to allow anyone to come and collect the dirty dishes. When one room filled up with used plates and glasses, he checked out of it and into a new one. On his death in 1875, the Earldom of Aldborough became extinct.

Sykes
Sir Tatton

Sir Tatton Sykes believed that the human body should be kept at a constant temperature. In order to achieve this himself he had a sequence of overcoats, each a different colour, made to fit over one another. Every morning he set out wearing several or all of them; as the day progressed, he shed them one by one. Rather than carrying his unwanted layers about with him, he just left them wherever they dropped and made a standing offer to the local children, a reward of one shilling for each coat returned to the house. He often wore two pairs of trousers for the same reason and was once seen in a railway carriage taking off his shoes and socks and sticking his feet out of the window in an effort to maintain the correct body temperature.

The tenants on the estate at Sledmere, in Yorkshire, got used to his appearance fairly quickly, but it must have taken them somewhat longer to come to terms with his views on the landscape. One of Sir Tatton's first acts on inheriting the property in 1863 was to plough up all the gardens and lawns on his property and to forbid the growing of flowers – 'nasty, untidy things' – in the village. He used his walking stick to knock down any offending blossoms which caught his eye and he advised one of his tenants, 'If you wish to grow flowers, grow cauliflowers!'

Sir Tatton also disliked people using their front doors and he forbade his tenants to do so. Their doors had to be barred or bolted and he had a number of houses built with *trompe-l'oeil* front doors and entrance possible only through the back. He also objected to gravestones, as a result of which the graves of members of Sykes's family who died during his 'reign' and were buried at Sledmere are unmarked and impossible to distinguish.

Sir Tatton travelled a great deal – to Japan, Mexico, Russia, China and America, as well as on the Continent. On these trips he took his cook with him, not so that he could indulge in spectacular meals but to ensure a continuous supply of milk puddings, the only really fit food for a delicate stomach.

One morning in 1911 Sledmere caught fire. Sir Tatton, warned to get out, stayed at table saying with his characteristic nervous stammer, 'First I must finish my pudding, finish my pudding.' Finally he emerged, settled into a chair on the front lawn and watched for eighteen hours as the old house was utterly destroyed. Rebuilding began at once, but when he died two years later, Sir Tatton was staying in London at the Metropole Hotel. The manager, fearful of the effect that this news might have on his other guests, wanted to smuggle the body out in a specially designed hollow sofa. Tatton's son Mark Sykes protested, 'However my father leaves this hotel, he shall leave it like a gentleman,' and his mortal remains were eventually carried out in a more conventional manner – though one suspects that the hotel manager's idea might have pleased the old man who left instructions that he was to be conveyed to his grave in a farm-cart.

Thompson
Margaret

hompson was first and foremost a lover of snuff. So strong was her fondness for this substance that when she died in 1776 she left instructions in her will that in the coffin her body be completely covered with the best Scotch snuff instead of flowers, since 'nothing can be so fragrant and refreshing to me as that precious powder'. As a preliminary to this she directed that her maid, Sarah Stuart, should line the coffin with all Miss Thompson's unwashed handkerchiefs.

No man was allowed to approach the open casket, but once closed it was carried by six men – the greatest snuff-takers in the parish of St James, Westminster – wearing snuff-coloured beaver hats rather than ordinary mourning clothes and six old maids wearing hoods and carrying a box of snuff to take for their refreshment as they went along.

The funeral procession was led by the minister, whom Miss Thompson desired to take on the way a certain quantity of the said snuff, not exceeding one pound. Sarah Stuart walked alongside him, tossing large handfuls of snuff to the crowds who followed behind. For those who did not attend the funeral, Miss Thompson left orders that two bushels of snuff be given away afterwards at her house.

Tyrrell
Lady Margaret-Ann

Lady Tyrrell, intelligent, charming and absent-minded, was far removed from the stereotype of the successful diplomat's wife. During Lord Tyrrell's time as British ambassador to Paris (1928–34) his wife showed no interest whatsoever in playing the grand hostess at official functions. In fact, she was rarely in Paris at all. Most of her time was devoted to research for a book on the history of the world, in which she intended to trace the development of all parts of the world from 2000 BC to the present, simultaneously.

167

On her infrequent visits to the French capital, Lady Tyrrell's favourite place of work was up a tree in the Embassy gardens. Here she sat in the branches, writing her book, and occasionally – when she wished to summon a footman – emitting a piercing whistle.

In the evenings she put aside her studies and attended formal dinner parties or receptions, where by all accounts her charm and wit made up for such minor confusions as mistaking the future George VI for her husband's private secretary or conversing for several hours with Lord Birkenhead under the impression that he was the Turkish Ambassador.

14th Baron Berners
Tyrwhitt-Wilson
Gerald Hugh

Posted at intervals on the fence surrounding an estate near Farringdon, Berkshire, were signs reading, 'DOGS WILL BE SHOT: CATS WILL BE WHIPPED.' Inside was Farringdon House, the home of Lord Berners, a gifted composer, artist, writer, and devisor of practical jokes. Visitors to Berners's home saw whippets wearing diamond collars, doves dyed all colours of the rainbow, and an impressive collection of automobiles, including an antique Rolls Royce with a clavichord built into the rear seat. One tea-party at Farringdon House consisted of Berners, Bubbles Radclyffe, Robert Heber-Percy, Penelope Chetwode, and her horse, a well-behaved beast, who went everywhere with his mistress.

From his house Berners could look across to the 140-foot high Farringdon Folly which he built in 1935. There was some public objection to the scheme when planning permission was sought. Asked to justify his request, Berners replied, 'The great point of the tower is that it will be entirely useless.' Somehow this reasoning convinced the authorities and the project was approved. The completed folly had a sign stating 'Members of the public committing suicide from this tower do so at their own risk.'

Ten years in the diplomatic service did not impair Berners's sense of humour. He took a dislike to a pompous senior member of chancery in one embassy who ended every statement by solemnly putting on his spectacles. With a piece of thread, Berners one day attached the spectacles to the ink bottle, blotter, letter-opener and several pens. Next time the spectacles were ritually raised to signal the end of a speech, most of the desk paraphernalia went with them.

Berners had a collection of other people's calling cards, of which he made judicious use. Having lent his house in Rome to a honeymooning couple, he sent the cards of London's most notorious bores on ahead to the butler with instructions to deliver one or two to the couple each day. The terrified honeymooners spent most of their stay taking elaborate precautions to avoid meeting the originals.

Berners himself had what he claimed was a foolproof technique for avoiding people or at least getting people to avoid him when travelling by railway. According to his friend, the painter Michael Ayrton, Berners, wearing a black skull-cap and black spectacles, would lean out of the window of his compartment at every stop and beckon passengers inside. This performance was usually enough to secure a private carriage, but if someone did dare to join him, they seldom stayed for long. In order to drive the intruder off, Berners pulled out the large clinical thermometer he travelled with and, with a worried expression on his face, began taking his temperature every five minutes. 'It was extraordinary,' Ayrton remarked, 'the way he could clear carriages by these simple means.'

As a composer of ballet and opera music, a landscape painter and a writer, Lord Berners was a serious, though never a solemn, artist. He had a reputation as a skilful parodist, even in his music and his painting. This trait is perhaps most evident in his satirical novels, one of which opens with this plea to the readers: 'The author will be obliged if his friends will not attempt to recognise each other in these pages.'

Urquhart
Sir Thomas

rquhart was knighted by Charles I in 1641 for his allegiance to the royalist cause. This loyalty resulted, ten years later, in Urquhart's imprisonment by Cromwell in the Tower of London. Although he was soon released on parole, his property was forfeited and the rest of his life was dominated by attempts to convince the government to restore his lands so that he could settle with his creditors. Even before his arrest Urquhart had demonstrated an interest in recondite knowledge and an unusual approach to language, two attributes that characterise all his later work. His *Trissotetras*, a trigonometrical treatise published in 1644, which, according to the *Encyclopedia Britannica*, is 'almost impenetrably obscure', contains a glossary that purports to explain such Urquhartisms as: 'Amfractuosities . . . the cranklings, windings, turnings, and involutions belonging to the equisoleary Scheme'; and 'Cathetobasall, is said of the Concordance of Loxogononsphericall Moods, in the Datas of the Perpendicular, and the Base, for finding out of the Maine question.'

The true flowering of Urquhart's creative genius, however came after his loss of property when he outdid himself in ingenuity in order to prove his worth to the state. He began with *Pantochrononchanon*, a genealogy of the Urquhart family, which Sir Thomas was able to trace back through 143 generations to 'the red earth from which God framed Adam', passing on the way such worthies as Methuselah, Noah, and Pamprosodos Urquhart, whose wife Termuth was the Pharaoh's daughter who found Moses in the bullrushes.

Having established his ancient lineage, Urquhart published one of his plans for the betterment of mankind, a universal language. In his announcement of the new language, Sir Thomas lists sixty-six advantages it possesses over existing tongues. Among these is the fact that his language has double the number of cases in most other languages, twelve parts of speech, eleven genders, ten tenses, and seven moods. Other advantages are: 'eighteenthly, each noun thereof, or verb, may begin or end with a vowel or a consonant, as to the peruser may seem most expedient . . . three and twentiethly, every word in this language signifieth as well backward as forward whereby a wonderful facility is obtained in making of anagrams.'

Urquhart never published the language itself (he said he would do so when his lands were returned), but he demonstrated his inventiveness with words in his life of the Scotsman, James Crichton, *The Admirable Crichton*, and in his translation of Rabelais's *Gargantua and Pantagruel*. In the latter, rather than following Rabelais's text literally, Urquhart delighted in expanding and indeed enriching the original. In one instance, as Richard Boston has pointed out in his biography of Urquhart, he enlarged a list of nine animal sounds to a catalogue of seventy-one, including the curking of quails, nuzzing of camels, smuttering of monkeys, charming of beagles, drintling of turkeys, boing of buffaloes, coniating of storks, gueriating of apes, and crouting of cormorants.

Towards the end of his life, unsuccessful in his efforts to restore his name, Urquhart left England. In 1660 he died abroad. Family tradition has it that his death was caused by an uncontrollable fit of laughter on hearing of the Restoration of Charles II.

Van Butchell
Martin

 an Butchell in his early days studied under William and John Hunter, two brothers who were among the most respected doctors of their time. Van Butchell trod a different path, however, and soon established himself as a highly fashionable dentist, able to charge as much as 80 guineas for a set of false teeth. He became popular not by toadying to the upper classes whose patronage he hoped to attract, but by bullying them and playing hard to get. His motto was 'I go to none' and he kept to it to the extent of once refusing an offer of 1000 guineas to make a house call.

He did not, however, feel it beneath him to insert curiously worded advertisements for himself in the papers, and in this way he achieved some notoriety. After a time dentistry lost its appeal for Van Butchell and he turned to the design and manufacture of trusses and other 'supports', in which enterprise he was also successful. Several contemporary satires of fashionable ladies show them wearing Van Butchell's garter.

But Van Butchell's real leap to fame came with the death of his first wife in January 1775. Van Butchell embalmed her with the aid of William Hunter, who injected a carmine dye into her blood vessels, imparting a rosy glow to her skin. She was provided with 'nicely matched glass eyes', dressed in a fine lace gown and laid out in the parlour in a glass-topped case. Why Van Butchell went to this trouble no one knows, but there was a rumour that a clause in the marriage settlement entitled him to his wife's fortune as long as she was above ground.

Whatever his reason, Van Butchell was soon besieged with people curious to have a look at what he always referred to as 'my dear departed'. Finally the crush got out of hand and he was forced to place an advertisement in the *St James Chronicle*, 21 October 1775: 'Van Butchell (not willing to be unpleasantly circumstanced and wishing to convince some good minds that they have been misinformed) acquaints the Curious, no stranger can see his embalmed wife, unless (by a Friend personally) introduced to himself, any day between Nine and One, Sundays excepted.'

The Curious would have found that Van Butchell was not

without some interesting features of his own. Shaving was against his principles, with the result that his beard hung down to his knees. Any hairs that fell out he sold at a guinea apiece as a sort of charm to help women who wanted children.

Van Butchell's favourite exercise was riding his grey pony, and large crowds often followed him on his outings. This may have been due to his penchant for painting the pony with purple spots or black stripes. Another personal oddity was his habit of always dining alone and his insistence that his wife and children do the same.

Although Van Butchell declared that the time during which his dear departed lay in state in the parlour was one of complete domestic bliss, he eventually chose a new wife. She, like her predecesor, was required by her husband at the outset of their married life to chose either black or white as the only colour in which she would henceforth appear. The first wife had chosen black; the second chose white. On one point, however, Van Butchell bowed to the demands of his new wife: the first Mrs Van Butchell was finally removed from public view. Her remains went to the Royal College of Surgeons. They were destroyed by enemy action in 1941.

Ward
John William

ard, an only child and heir to one of the largest fortunes in England, had an upbringing which was designed to set him above his peers in education and accomplishment. It was more successful, however, in setting him apart emotionally. When he was still a child, a house was set up for him in London, away from his friends and family and there he lived with only his tutors for company. The result was an elegant, introverted boy who was destined to live alone. He was not a recluse, however, and after Oxford he stood for Parliament and made something of a name for himself as a dandy and wit. Byron called him 'studious, brilliant, elegant and sometimes piquant'. He served briefly as foreign minister under Canning. During his tenure he exhibited beautifully that absent-mindedness for which he was famous. Shortly before the Battle of Navarino in 1827, Ward thoughtlessly put a letter to the French ambassador into an envelope addressed to the Russian ambassador, Prince Lieven. When he received the letter, Prince Lieven, who was a consummate diplomatic schemer, saw at once that Ward had perpetrated an ingenious, sinister plot to try and confuse the Russians with false information. He returned the letter – unread he said – congratulating himself on his narrow escape and praising Ward's clever ruse all over London.

Many of the stories about Ward centre on his habit of talking to himself. At a dinner party, for example, he would rehearse his *bons mots*, as he thought, under his breath, but his mutterings were clearly audible to those near him, who therefore heard all his witticisms at least twice. The two voices – one shrill and one gruff – that he used in conducting conversations with himself, were said to sound like Lord Dudley conversing with Lord Ward. He seemed entirely unaware that his thoughts were being overheard. Presumably he did not even have the satisfaction of realising that all London was delighted by his muttered reaction to a much-disliked man who offered to walk Ward from the Commons to the Travellers Club: 'I don't suppose it will bore me *very* much to let him walk with me that distance.'

174

As he grew older his absent-mindedness increased and he often seemed to forget where he was. Dining at the house of a woman who prided herself in serving the best food in London, Ward apologised to the other guests for the poor quality of the meal, but explained 'my cook isn't feeling well'. Another time Ward paid a call and after sitting for more than the required length of time and failing to respond to his hostess's repeated hints that he should leave, he muttered, 'a very pretty woman, but she stays a devilish long time. I wish she'd go.'

Eventually Ward's loneliness became too much of a strain for him and, possibly after a rejection by the Earl of Beverly's daughter, he invented a wife for himself, speaking of her with great affection. In 1832 he behaved so strangely at one of his own dinner parties that a doctor who was present had him confined. He later suffered a paralytic stroke and died in 1833.

Waring
Francis

At the beginning of every service, Francis Waring, vicar of Heybridge in Essex since 1798, set a small clock on a ledge in front of him. He then read the lessons at breakneck speed, allowing the congregation no time to make the responses; gave a brief sermon, not much longer than a proverb; ran down the aisle; jumped on a horse and rushed off to take services at two nearby churches.

Waring appeared in church in various odd hats and vestments of his own devising. When his bishop tried to remonstrate with him for wearing purple dress at an ecclesiastical gathering, Waring smiled broadly and held out a card. 'How very good of you to notice. Do let me recommend my tailor to you.' His wardrobe had to be extensive to permit him to change outfits three or more times a day according to his mood. He was fond of dressing like a Quaker. To please him, his wife obligingly wore a grey and white Quaker costume every Wednesday.

Waring's domestic arrangements were dictated by his own obscure but strongly held principles. Insisting that every house should have a central passageway, he rebuilt his to obtain one. None the less he deliberately made it so narrow that it could accommodate only one person at a time. As Waring was not a small man, anyone meeting him in the corridor had to step into a doorway to let him pass. He was not poor but he furnished his house with rough logs rather than chairs. The children fed from a trough. Waring and his wife slept in a huge wicker rocking-cradle. Each member of the household was assigned his or her own distinctive sound, like a bird-call, which Waring whistled to summon them.

Waring's sense of humour made him popular in Heybridge, though his tendency to irreverence upset a few parishioners. One incident that did a great deal for his standing in the community was his run-in with the much disliked mayor of the neighbouring village of Maldon, Mr Bugg. A pompous man with a marked resemblance to a bulldog, Bugg was pointedly rude to the vicar at a public dinner. To the intense delight of onlookers, Waring simply looked Bulldog Bugg in the face and barked.

Warner
Henry Lee

If, while taking his usual midnight stroll, Henry Lee Warner of Walsingham Abbey, Norfolk, chanced to see someone cutting branches off one of the trees on his estate, he took immediate action. 'Take care how you get down that tree or you may hurt yourself', he would call out softly so as not to startle the poacher. The local people called Warner 'too good', and at one time or other most of the villagers had a go at plundering his land. He simply could not bring himself to take action against anybody, no matter how much damage was inflicted on his estate. The pillaging went on in broad daylight as well as at night. By the end of his life in 1802 his extensive woods were reduced to barely a dozen lonely trees.

Warner slept all day, rising late in the evening to concentrate on his scholarly pursuits, and dining at four in the morning. He saw little company because of his odd hours, so his out-of-date costume – gold-laced coat, lace neckcloth and curve-toed shoes, all fashionable fifty years ago in his youth – was not much noticed.

It must have seemed to Warner's neighbours that he went out

of his way to make himself and his possessions vulnerable. It was well known that he chose to forfeit £500 rather than agree to serve as Sheriff of Norfolk, a role which he feared might require him to pass judgment or inflict punishment on local criminals. Although he seldom rode, Warner kept a stable; and anyone was free to borrow his horses, saddles, harnesses, etc. for a day or a fortnight with no questions asked. It is doubtful whether his indulgence had a beneficial effect on his neighbours; eventually they became so dependent on the easy pickings of Warner's land that they disdained to steal his grain until it had been cut and neatly stacked.

Waterton
Charles

In May 1829 Charles Waterton, squire of Walton Hall, Yorkshire, took his seventeen-year-old bride on a European honeymoon. It was a thrill for her to visit Paris, Antwerp and Ghent in the company of a man of the world after years of a restrictive convent education. And Charles made sure his young wife saw all the highlights – they visited virtually every significant collection of stuffed animals and birds in Northern Europe.

Of course to anyone who knew Charles at all well, a category which most likely did not include his bride Anne, such a honeymoon would not have been surprising. His interest in collecting and preserving birds and animals began with his journeys in the South American jungle. Waterton, who had his own technique for preserving interesting specimens in a lifelike condition, made his home into a museum with exhibits such as 'The English Reformation Zoologically Demonstrated', a series of 'portraits' of famous Protestants (Waterton was a militant Catholic) fashioned from preserved toads, lizards, and other loathsome creatures. He also exhibited something he called the Nondescript. This was a Red Howler monkey whose face had been manipulated into a startlingly human cast which fooled, horrified, or offended most viewers. Besides these and other freaks – such as albino hedgehogs – inside the house, there were numerous items of interest outdoors in the park. Waterton turned Walton Hall into the first refuge for wild birds, surrounding it with three miles of high wall to keep out predators. Poachers were confounded by the seventy or eighty wooden pheasants scattered in lifelike poses throughout the woods.

Waterton always kept a fire going in the house, no matter what the weather. Even outdoors he built a fire if he was staying in one place for more than a few minutes. This self-indulgence was unusual for he lived according to a strict regimen, going to bed at 8 p.m. and rising at 3.30 in the morning, with a half-hour break in his sleep for prayers at midnight. After his wife's death in childbirth in their first year of marriage, Waterton always slept on the floor with only a wooden block for a pillow.

Bleeding himself – 'tapping my claret' as he called it – was almost a hobby with Waterton. He did it over a hundred times, often taking 16 to 20 ounces, right up to the end of his life. In order to learn more about vampire bats on one of his South American expeditions he slept for weeks with his foot hanging out of the hammock and was terribly disappointed when 'the provoking brute' failed to bite him.

This way of life must have agreed with him, for in his eightieth year he was still astonishing visitors who caught a glimpse of him scampering up a tall tree or calmly scratching 'the back part of his head with the big toe of his right foot'. When Waterton's great friend and biographer, Dr Richard Hobson came to Walton Hall, he was often greeted by a playful nip on the ankles from his host who bounded out to meet him on all fours, barking.

Without a doubt Waterton's main contribution to knowledge was his collection of the potent arrow poison, curare, in the South American jungle, and his demonstration – which entailed giving artificial respiration to a donkey – that it could safely be used as a muscle relaxant. The donkey lived on for almost twenty-five years at Walton Hall. After her death Waterton sent her obituary to the *St James Chronicle*.

Waterton had strong opinions on the matter of dress. Comfort and convenience were of prime importance. Very wide trousers, loose shoes, and a hat with air vents (since like Francis Galton (*q.v.*) he believed a head should breathe), were his everyday wear. He wrote an essay titled 'Tight Shoes, Tight Stays, and Cravats', setting forth in no uncertain terms his views on these sartorial perversions. He also refused to wear evening clothes, which was probably just as well since his crew-cut hair (not a very common nineteenth-century style) might have spoiled the effect.

178

The Squire of Walton Hall was generous, but naive. After a number of incidents in which an ostensibly needy applicant for a portion of the Waterton largesse was discovered to be a notorious drunkard or layabout, Charles was persuaded to stop dispensing cash and took instead to giving out tokens redeemable at local shops for shoes and food.

In 1817 Waterton had a run-in with the Pope Pius VII. He and a friend, visiting Rome, scaled the facade of St Peter's and put their gloves on top of the lightning conductor. The Pope was furious and ordered the gloves removed. Only one person could be found willing to make this dangerous ascent and placate the pontiff: the devout Catholic, Charles Waterton.

'The Scottish Homer'

Wilkie
William

The poet William Wilkie was once asked by Lady Lauderdale, the wife of his patron, to stay the night with them. Wilkie replied that he would stay on condition that her ladyship supply him with a pair of dirty sheets. Wilkie absolutely refused to sleep between clean sheets; and if he did have the misfortune to encounter a pair always removed them before getting into bed. A blanket was the only thing he cared for. Well, not *a* blanket, exactly, since he covered himself with twenty-four pairs of blankets every night.

Wilkie, who had taken holy orders, was very absent-minded. He often forgot to remove his hat while preaching and more than once left the church before the service was over even though he was officiating. On one occasion he forgot to consecrate the bread and wine before distributing communion.

Although he was a learned man, Wilkie read very badly and could not spell. He was dubbed the 'Scottish Homer' after the publication in 1757 of his *Epigoniad*, an epic poem in the style of the *Iliad*. Tradition has it that Wilkie consulted only one person while writing the poem: he read each section aloud to an old village woman, Margaret Paton, changing and rewriting whatever she did not like until the whole had received her blessing.

Wilson
George

George Wilson began his working life as a shoemaker. He then spent seven years helping his mother in her pawnbroker's shop. From there he went on to become a linen draper, a hosier and, finally, a tax collector. None of these occupations particularly suited him, but as a tax collector, obliged to track his quarry over long distances, he discovered his flair for pedestrianism. Wilson often walked 50 or 60 miles a day with no ill effects and made the trip from Newcastle to London, a distance of 274 miles, in four days.

Before long his talent was recognised by a publisher who employed him to help prepare an *Itinerary of Great Britain*; Wilson's job was to verify the distances between various points by walking the routes himself. After that venture he continued to walk around northern England and Scotland, supporting himself by selling pamphlets and maps along the way. At this time Wilson became involved with an unscrupulous business partner who absconded and left him responsible for several large debts. Mostly through his wife's machinations – she wanted him out of the way so that she could, so to speak, pursue her own affairs – he was thrown into jail.

Here Wilson entered into the second phase of his careers: walking set distances for wagers or subscriptions. In jail he walked 50 miles in twelve hours, although the yard measured only 33 by 25½ feet. On another occasion, when he was free, he covered 109 miles in twenty-four hours. Later he moved to London and made his living by distributing the morning papers in Kent.

In 1809 the great pedestrian Captain Barclay had won fame by walking 1000 miles in 1000 hours. At the age of forty Wilson proposed to go one better by covering the same distance in twenty days, less than half the time. He set out from the Hare and Billet in Blackheath at 5.30 a.m. on II September 1815. The plan was to walk back and forth between the pub and a point one half mile up the road, covering 50 miles a day. On Sunday mornings he would rest from his labours, completing his allotted 50 miles later in the day. At the end of each day Wilson was transported to his sleeping quarters in a sedan-chair and his feet bathed in salt water.

Spectators soon gathered along his route and within a few days a carnival atmosphere had developed, aided by the presence of tents, booths, games, food, dancing, and rows of carriages and carts carrying families out for a day in the country. Wilson was courteous to the crowd – never failing to raise his hat to the ladies – but enthusiastic supporters pressing in on him threatened to block his progress until a path was roped off for him.

On Tuesday, 26 September, with Wilson only five days and 250 miles from his goal, the Blackheath magistrates placed him under house arrest for disturbing the peace. Wilson protested that he had given due notice of his plan to walk and that he was not responsible for the assembled crowds, but the magistrates refused to alter their views. Wilson's friends, furious about this turn of events, managed to raise several hundred pounds by subscription, to compensate the disappointed pedestrian. The next morning Wilson, resigned to his fate, calmed his nerves by taking a long walk on the heath.

Wingate
Orde

By the time of his tragic death in 1944 in an aeroplane crash in Burma at the age of forty-one, Orde Wingate had established himself as one of the most successful and unorthodox tacticians in the British army and a scourge of the military establishment. Throughout his career he delighted in flouting authority. His individuality expressed itself both in his brilliant guerrilla campaigns in Burma and Ethiopia and in his contemptuous refusal to abide by social convention.

In spite of a puritan upbringing which left him with a mystical obsession with the Old Testament, Wingate had a disconcerting habit of receiving callers and conducting strategy sessions in the nude. Military colleagues grew accustomed to this in time, but Eliahu Elath, the future Israeli ambassador to the Court of St James, was somewhat flustered to find himself engaged in an intense discussion about Zionism with a completely naked man.

Things could have been worse. It was only later that Wingate decided that bathing was unhealthy. Once he adopted that theory, callers like Leonard Mosley, on one occasion in Khartoum, were likely to find their host not only naked, but diligently brushing his body clean with a tooth-brush throughout the interview. All discussion came abruptly to an end when the miniature alarm clock he wore on his little finger indicated that the time was up. Breaking off in the middle of a sentence, if necessary, Wingate would rise and escort his visitor to the door. Of course he did not always greet callers in a state of undress. He had a special uniform reserved for VIP occasions. It was covered with grease stains and expressed to perfection his disdain for considerations of rank.

Wingate maintained that every man should be his own doctor. One of his theories about health in the tropics was that eating half a dozen raw onions a day was the best way to stay fit. Sometimes he ate nothing but onions and grapes for days at a time.

An interest in the Old Testament helped to convert Wingate to Zionism, and on occasion even influenced his military tactics. During the Arab rebellion against Jewish resettlement in Palestine, he decided to take an Arab-held village using Gideon's method of frightening the enemy into flight by having all his men blow on rams's horns. An order was placed for a shipment of rams's horns, but to Wingate's fury only bugles were available. These proved ineffective and, perhaps luckily, no further opportunity arose for testing Gideon's tactics.

Wintle
Alfred Daniel

'I get down on my knees every night and thank God for making me English.' Lt Col. A D Wintle of the First Royal Dragoons, the self-proclaimed quintessential Englishman and author of the above words, was born in Russia and educated in France and Germany. He was, however, a British citizen – the son of a diplomat – and an ardent chauvinist from his youth.

After attending the Royal Military Academy at Woolwich, Wintle joined the cavalry with the intention of being on horseback as much as possible: 'Time spent dismounted', he solemnly warned readers of his autobiography, 'can never be regained.' Even in the army Wintle took care to furnish himself with the true Englishman's basic equipment, a monocle and an umbrella. For the former, Wintle scorned the safety device of a cord or chain, trusting instead to the security of a determined squint to keep his eyepiece in position. The umbrella ('no gentleman ever leaves home without it') was never opened ('no true gentleman ever unfurls his umbrella') except to insert a note reading, 'This umbrella stolen from Col. A D Wintle.'

Wintle's career in the First War was marked by extra-ordinary acts of bravery and a persistent indignation with the misjudgments of his superiors. His diary for 19 June 1919 reads, 'Great War Peace signed at last'; the next day he wrote, 'I declare private war on Germany.' He fulminated against the authorities for refusing to accept his conviction that a second war with Germany in the near future was inevitable. He was disgusted with the War Office, whose *raison d'être*, in Wintle's opinion, was to look forward to and plan for the next war.

When that war started, Wintle was determined to go to France. As usual his superior officers would not oblige. Wintle tried everything: he plotted to leave the army and go over on his own; he attempted to commandeer a military aeroplane to fly him to France. None of his schemes worked. Finally in desperation he pulled a gun on an official at the Air Ministry and demanded to be sent. Naturally, this action did not meet with a favourable response. Wintle then accused the official and several members of the government of grave mismanagement of the war effort and emptied his revolver into the man's desk.

In the Tower of London, awaiting court-martial, Wintle lived in style, with a Guardsman as his personal servant, a formal dinner every evening and visitors to tea and lunch. At the court-martial, the government was so embarrassed by Wintle's accusations that most of the charges against him were dropped and he received only a reprimand. Eventually he was sent abroad.

In 1941 Wintle was captured as a spy in occupied France. He escaped once, was betrayed and reimprisoned. Back in jail, Wintle went on a hunger strike for two weeks in protest at the slovenly appearance and off-hand behaviour of his guards who, he said, were not fit to guard a British officer. He held daily inspections and berated them for their unmilitary deportment and their low treachery in supporting the Vichy regime.

After the war Wintle retired to Wrotham with his wife and

devoted himself to writing novels and fighting to maintain the English way of life. In an incident to touch the hearts of all commuters, Wintle once boarded a train at Victoria, having purchased a first-class ticket, only to discover that all the seats were taken. Realising that 'I had to teach British Railways a lesson', Wintle took the driver's seat and refused to move until another coach was added to the train. He had his way.

In 1948 Wintle embarked on a ten-year battle to wrest the small fortune left by his maiden cousin, Kitty, out of what he regarded as the wrong hands. Kitty left the bulk of her estate to her solicitor, a man called Frederick Nye. Wintle believed that the money was intended for two other members of her family. In an attempt to get Nye into court, Wintle lured him to a flat in Hove, debagged him, and sent photographic evidence of the deed to the newspapers. The plot backfired – though it is hard to imagine how Wintle ever believed it would help his case – and Wintle was sentenced to and served six months in Wormwood Scrubs. Acting as his own lawyer, Wintle took his case against the will right up to the House of Lords. After a hearing that lasted for six days, the Lords gave unanimous decision in Wintle's favour, the first such decision in support of a layman conducting his own case.

When, in 1966, Wintle died, *The Times* devoted a leader to him, praising his 'impractical and uncomfortable' eccentricity as a mark of character and individuality. But the greatest tribute to Wintle had come seven years earlier in an episode of the television programme, 'This Is Your Life', devoted to him. Maurice Molia, the head of the garrison in Vichy France responsible for guarding Wintle during the war, appeared on the programme to say that 'entirely because of Wintle's dauntless example and his tirade of abuse and challenge', Molia and 280 of the garrison's men had gone over to the Resistance during the War.

Eccentric Bibliography

Aldington, Richard, *The Strange Life of Charles Waterton*, London 1949.

Alsop, Susan, *Lady Sackville*, London 1976.

Angelo, Henry, *Reminiscences*, London 1828, 1830.

Apperley, C J, *Life of John Mytton*, London 1871.

Askwith, Betty, *Two Victorian Families*, London 1977.

Baring-Gould, Sabine, *Yorkshire Oddities*, 1890.

Barker, E H, *Porsoniana*, London 1852.

Barnes, Allsion, *Essex Eccentrics*, Ipswich 1975.

Barrington, Sir Jonah, *Personal Sketches of His Own Time*, London 1869.

Bentinck, W J A (6th Duke of Portland), *Men, Women and Things*, London 1937.

Besterman, T, *The Druce-Portland Case*, London 1935.

Biddulph, Violet, *Kitty, Duchess of Queensberry*, London 1935.

Biographica Brittanica, London 1747–93.

Blunt, Wilfred, *John Christie of Glyndebourne*, London 1968.

Boase, Frederic, *Modern English Biography*, Truro 1892–1921.

Boston, Richard, *The Admirable Urquhart*, London 1975.

Brande, W T, *The Life and Adventures of the Celebrated Walking Stewart*, London 1822.

Brendon, Piers, *Hawker of Morwenstow*, London 1975.

Bridgeman, Harriet and Drury, Elizabeth (eds), *The British Eccentrics*, London 1975.

Burke, Sir John B, *Families of Ireland*, London 1976.

Burke, Sir John B, *Romance of the Aristocracy*, London 1855.

Burke, Sir John B, *Vicissitudes of Families*, London 1859.

Burgess, G H O, *The Curious World of Frank Buckland*, London 1967.

Caulfield, James, *Portraits of Remarkable Persons*, London 1794, 1819.

Chambers, Robert, *The Book of Days*, London 1863–4.

Chambers, Robert, *Biographical Dictionary of Eminent Scotsmen*, Edinburgh 1848.

Chambers, Robert, *Traditions of Edinburgh*, Edinburgh 1825.

Champion de Crespigny, Sir Claude, *Memoirs*, London 1896.

Chapman, G, *Life of Beckford*, London 1937.

Cochrane, A D R, *In the Days of the Dandies*, Edinburgh 1890.

Cokayne, G E, *The Complete Peerage*, London 1887–1938.

De Quincey, Thomas, *Autobiography*, London 1889.

Dictionary of National Biography, Oxford 1975.

Florence, P S (ed.), *C.K. Ogden: a collective memoir*, London 1977.

Faringdon, Joseph, *The Faringdon Diary*, James Greig (ed.), London 1922–28.

Fothergill, Brian, *Beckford of Fonthill*, London 1979.

Galton, F, *The Art of Travel*, London 1855.

Gantz, Ida, *Signpost to Eyrecourt*, 1975.

Garrett, Richard, *They Must Have Been Crazy*, London 1977.

George, Mary D, *Catalogue of Political and Personal Satires in the British Museum*, London.

Goffin, Magdalen, *Maria Pasqua*, London 1979.

Gordon, E O, *Life of William Buckland*, London 1894.

Gower, Granville Leverson, *Private Correspondence*, London 1916.

Greville, Charles C F, *The Greville Diary*, London 1818–1856.

Gronow, Captain Rees Howell, *Reminiscences*, London 1881.

Hangar, George, *The Life, Adventures and Opinions of Col. G.H.Hangar*, London 1801.

Hearne, Thomas, *Reliquiae Hearnianae*, P Bliss (ed.), Oxford 1857.

Hine, Reginald, *Hitchin Worthies*, London 1932.

Humphreys, A L, *Eccentric Characters of Berkshire*, Reading 1926.

Jones, Barbara, *Follies and Grottoes*, London 1974.

Kay, John, *Edinburgh Portraits*, Edinburgh 1885.

Kennedy, Carol, *Eccentric Soldiers*, London 1975.

Kirby, R S, *Wonderful and Eccentric Museum*, London 1815.

Lancaster, Sir Obsert, *With An Eye To The Future*, London 1967.

Lewson, Jane, *A True and Wonderful Account of Jane Lewson*, London 1816.

Loudan, J, *O Rare Amanda*, London 1954.

McGonagall, William, *Poetic Gems*, London 1934.

Masters, Brian, *The Dukes*, London 1975.

Melville, Lewis, *Some Eccentrics and A Woman*, London 1911.

Morris, Jan, *The Oxford Book of Oxford*, 1978.

Newburgh, Brockhill, *Essays*, Dublin 1769.

Old Edinburgh Peddlers and Beggars, Edinburgh 1886.

Pevsner, Nikolaus, *Buildings of England*, Harmondsworth 1951–79.

Phillips, D, *No Poet's Corner in the Abbey*, Dundee 1971.

Redding, Cyrus, *Past Celebrities Whom I Have Known*, London 1866.

Redding Cyrus, *Memoirs of Remarkable Misers*, London 1863.

Robinson, J R and H H, *Life of Robert Coates*, London 1891.

Rogers, Charles, *Traits of Scottish People*, Edinburgh 1867.

Russell, G W E, *Collections and Recollections*, London 1898.

Sackville-West, Vita, *Pepita*, London 1937.

Sanders, C R, *The Strachey Family*, 1953.

Seward, Anna, *Memoirs of Darwin*, 1804.

Sheridan, Thomas, *Life of Swift*, London 1787.

Sitwell, Edith, *English Eccentrics*, London 1933.
Sitwell, Sir Osbert, *Left Hand, Right Hand!*, London 1945–50.
Smith, J T, *A Book for a Rainy Day*, London 1818.
Smythe, Dame Ethel, *Maurice Baring*, London 1938.
Somerville-Large Peter, *Irish Eccentrics*, London 1975.
Spencer, Herbert, *Home Life with Herbert Spencer, by Two*, London 1906.
Sykes, Christopher, *Orde Wingate*, London 1959.
Sykes, Christopher Simon, *The Visitor's Book*, London 1978.
Timbs, John, *English Eccentrics and Eccentricities*, London 1877.
Topham, Major Edward, *Life of John Elwes*, London 1790.
Victoria History of the Counties of England, Oxford 1900.
Walpole, Horace, *Letters*, P Toynbee (ed.), Oxford (1903–25).
Waterton, Charles, *Wanderings in South America*, London 1825.
Watson, John S, *Life of Porson*, London 1861.
Wilson, Henry, *The Book of Wonderful Characters*, London 1869.
Wilson, Henry, *The Eccentric Mirror*, London 1813.
Wintle, Col. A D, *The Last Englishman*, London 1966.
Wraxall, Sir N W, *Historical Memoirs*, London 1884.
Wykes, Alan, *Eccentric Doctors*, London 1975.

Newspapers and Periodicals

'The Annual Register', London 1758–1919.
'The Book Collector', Winter 1979.
'Cork Historical and Archeological Journal', 1892.
'Dublin University Magazine', vol. xviii.
Eastern Evening News, 15 November 1961; 30 January 1969.
'Gentleman's Magazine'.
Illustrated London News.
The *Listener*.
Monthly Magazine, July 1802.
Notes and Queries.
'Proceedings of the British Academy'.
Rochdale Observer, 1976.
The *Spectator*.
The Times.

List of Dates

Alington, *John* 1795–1863
Badger, *Harry* fl. early 19th century
Bagenal, *Beauchamp* 1741–1802
Baring, *Maurice* 1874–1945
Barrett, *John* 1753–1821
Barrett-Lennard, *Sir Thomas* 1826–1919
Beauclerk, *Osborne de Vere, 12th Duke of St Albans* 1875–1964
Beckford, *William* 1759–1844
Bentham, *Jeremy* 1748–1832 (*see under* Ogden)
Bentinck-Scott, *William John Cavendish, 5th Duke of Portland* 1800–1879
Beswick, *Hannah* 1680–1758
Bigg, *John, 'The Dinton Hermit'* 1629–1696
Birch, *Thomas* 1705–1766
Blackhurst, *Ivy Mabel* 1894–1975
Bowles, *Thomas Gibson* 1842–1922
Britton, *Thomas* c. 1654–1714
Brudenell, *Adeline, Countess of Cardigan* 1825–1915
Buckland, *Francis Trevelyan* 1826–1880
Buckland, *William* 1784–1856
Burnett, *James, Lord Monboddo* 1714–1799
Capper, *Joseph* 1727–1804
Cavendish, *Hon.Henry* 1731–1810
Champion de Crespigny, *Sir Claude* 1847–1935
Christie, *John* 1882–1962
Coates, *Robert* 1772–1848
Cope, *Henry* c. 1735–1806
Curtis, *James* fl. 1834
Cussans, *William* fl. 1796
Dancer, *Daniel* 1716–1794
Davy, *Sir Humphrey* 1778–1829 (*see under* Birch)
Day, *Thomas* 1748–1789
Densham, *F W* d. 1953
Dering, *George Edward* 1831–1911
Digweed, *Ernest* 1895–1976
Dinely-Goodere, *Sir John* 1739–1808
Douglas, *Alexander Hamilton, 10th Duke of Hamilton* 1767–1852
Douglas, *Catherine, Duchess of Queensberry* 1700–1777
Duff, *Jamie* d. 1788
Egerton, *Francis Henry, 8th Earl of Bridgewater* 1756–1829
Ellerton, *Simeon* 1694–1799
Elwes, *Sir Harvey* d. 1763
Elwes, *John* 1714–1789

Eyre, *Edward* c. 1759–1803
Eyre, *Giles* 1766–1830
Eyre, *John, Lord Eyre of Eyrecourt* 1720–1781
Fitzgerald, *John* 1803–1879
Fordyce, *George* 1736–1802
Fuller, *John* 1757–1834
Gainsborough, *Jack* 1711–1788
Galton, *Sir Francis* 1822–1911
Graham, *James* 1745–1794
Halstead, *John* 1868–1940
Hamilton, *Charles* 1703–1786
Hamilton, *John James, Marquess of Abercorn* 1756–1818
Hamilton, *Robert* 1743–1829
Hanger, *George, Baron Coleraine* 1751–1824
Hardy, *Godfrey Harold* 1887–1947
Hawker, *Robert* 1803–1875
Hirst, *Jemmy* 1738–1829
James, *Venetia* 1855–1939
Jennings, *Henry Constantine* 1731–1819
Jones, *Morgan* fl. 1781–1824
Kirwan, *Richard* 1733–1812
Kitchiner, *William*, 1775–1827
Kolkhurst, *George Alfred* 1897–1958
Langford, *Mr* d. 1804
Lole, *William* 1800–1874
Lowther, *Sir James, Earl of Lonsdale* 1736–1802
Lucas, *James* 1813–1874
McGonagall, *William* 1825–1902
Maguire, *Brian* d. 1835
Mathew, *George* d. 1738
Matthewson, *R N* fl. 1912
Maturin, *Charles Robert* 1782–1824
Mytton, *John* 1796–1834
Neild, *James Camden* 1780–1852
Noailles, *Helena Comtesse de* 1824–1908
Norton, *Joshua* 1819–1880
Ogden, *Charles Kay* 1889–1957
Pockrich, *Richard* c. 1690–1759
Porson, *Richard* 1759–1808
Pottesman, *Solomon* 1904–1978
Robertson, *James* d. 1790
Robinson, *Matthew, 2nd Baron Rokeby 1712–1800*
Ros, *Amanda McKettrick* 1860–1939
Sackville-West, *Victoria-Josefa, Baroness Sackville* 1862–1936
Seymour, *Charles, 6th Duke of Somerset* 1662–1748
Simpson, *F A* 1883–1974 (*see under* Hardy)
Sitwell, *Sir George Reresby* 1860–1943

Skeffington, *Clotworthy, 2nd Earl of Masserene* 1742–1805
Spence, *Thomas* 1750–1814
Spencer, *Herbert* 1820–1903
Stanhope, *Charles, Lord Petersham, 4th Earl of Harrington* 1780–1851
Stewart, *John* 1749–1822
Strachey, *William* 1819–1904
Stratford, *Benjamin O'Neale II, 6th Earl of Aldborough* 1808–1875
Stratford, *Edward Augustus, 2nd Earl of Aldborough* d. 1801
Stratford, *John, 1st Earl of Alborough* 1689–1777
Stratford, *John, 3rd Earl of Alborough* d. 1823
Sykes, *Sir Tatton* 1826–1913
Thompson, *Margaret* d. 1776
Tyrrell, *Lady Margaret-Ann* d. 1939
Tyrwhitt-Wilson, *Gerald Hugh, 14th Baron Berners* 1883–1950
Urquhart, *Sir Thomas* 1611–1660
Van Butchell, *Martin* 1735–c. 1812
Ward, *John William, 4th Viscount Dudley and Ward and 1st Earl of
    Dudley* 1781–1833
Waring, *Francis* d. 1833
Warner, *Henry Lee* 1722–1802
Waterton, *Charles* 1782–1865
Wilkie, *William* 1721–1772
Wilson, *George* fl. 1815
Wingate, *Orde* 1903–1944
Wintle, *Alfred Daniel* 1897–1966